The training of judges and public prosecutors in Europe

proceedings

Multilateral meeting
organised by the Council of Europe
in conjunction with the Centre
for Judicial Studies, Lisbon

Lisbon, 27-28 April 1995

Themis Plan 3

Council of Europe legal co-operation with
central and eastern European countries

Council of Europe Publishing

French edition:
La formation des juges et des magistrats du parquet en Europe
ISBN 92-871-3015-9

Council of Europe Publishing
F-67075 Strasbourg Cedex

ISBN 92-871-3016-7
© Council of Europe, 1996
Printed in Germany

Contents

Opening speech by Mr Armando LEANDRO........5

Requirements for admission to the professions of judge and public prosecutor - selection criteria and means of recruitment - comparative examination

Mr Johann-Friedrich STAATS (Germany) 9

Mrs Ána Maria PÉREZ TÓRTOLA (Spain) 13

Mr Fernando ESCRIBANO MORA (Spain) 17

Mr Daniel LUDET (France) 19

Mr Joep J.I. VERBURG (Netherlands) 23

Mr Armando LEANDRO (Portugal) 27

Mr Ian CAMPBELL (United Kingdom) 31

M. Stanislaw WALTOŚ (Pologne) 35

Basic training: content and methods, duration of the various phases

Mrs Maud VIGNAU (France) 41

Mr Joep J.I. VERBURG (Pays-Bas) 47

Mr José António MESQUITA (Portugal) 51

In-service training: content, methods and evaluation of results

Mr Helmut PALDER (Allemagne) 57

Mr José de la MATA AMAYA (Espagne) 65

Mr Daniel LECRUBIER (France) 73

Mr Joep J.I. VERBURG (Pays-Bas) 79

Mr Armando LEANDRO (Portugal) 83

CONCLUSIONS 85

Preparatory questionnaire 89

Synthesis of the answers to the questionnaire 93

Comparative tables 157

Programme 173

List of participants 177

OPENING SPEECH

by Armando LEANDRO
Director of the Centro de Estudos Judiciáros

Ladies and gentlemen,

I would like to begin by welcoming you on behalf of the *Centro de Estudos Judiciáros* and saying how gratified and honoured we are to host this meeting, the purpose of which is to exchange information and ideas on the training of judges and public prosecutors. This is a highly topical issue and a key one in the complex societies at the height of their transition and the eventful times in which we are living.

We are all aware of the crucial role of the law in establishing, handing down and securing the fundamental values of a democratic society and appreciate the key importance in our society of:

- the administration of justice as a necessary function of the State;

- the independence of the courts;

- applying the law in such a way that it primarily benefits the people to whom it is addressed, namely the citizens;

- accentuating the role of the judiciary as a guarantee of the fundamental values which democratic societies adopt as elements of a pluralist way of life.

In line with this democratic requirement the judiciary must:

- provide effective protection for the rights and interests of citizens protected under law;

- settle disputes;

- ensure compliance with the constitution whilst safeguarding basic values;

- encourage re-interpretation of these values in line with social changes and new historic realities.

The judiciary must ensure that justice is close to the people albeit without going against the principle of legal certainty and thus encourage:

- a forward- and not a backward-looking interpretation of the law;

- an interpretation which stems from an ongoing effort to achieve the goals which have been set and takes account of legal and social changes;

- effective implementation of the law in accordance with the real needs of the individual.

The judiciary has a duty to provide — by asserting its maturity and displaying its awareness of its genuine independence with respect to the other authorities, as well as by recognising its role as a counterbalance in a society which is still closed and distrustful — the basis for constructive dialogue and co-operation with the various other structures whose role is also to serve the public and the community, thus rendering the transition towards an open and trustful society easier.

All of this points to the need for exacting training for judges and prosecutors from the ethical, technical and cultural points of view.

Much stress will be placed on the notion of increasing professionalism by means of thorough selection and initial and in-service training which places a premium on forming the judges' and prosecutors' characters — training which does not just provide them with technical skills and knowledge, but also:

- develops their "life skills";

- enhances their sense of responsibility, and

- helps them to bear in mind the social and human repercussions of their judgments with a view to efficiency with a non-technocratic, humanist face.

Although the training of judges and prosecutors has an ethical, moral and technical side, it also reflects the varying notions of public service of different countries and is therefore characterised by various slight differences that reflect the social, economic and cultural context of each country.

However, the value of exchanging ideas and sharing experiences relating to the goals, the content and the methodology of training is clear.

Accordingly, it is obvious what benefits can be brought by establishing channels of communication and various forms of co-operation enabling each system to be improved through knowledge of the principles, experiences and assessments of other systems.

This is the goal of this meeting.

Please allow me to express our gratification that this meeting is being held under the auspices of the Council of Europe, which has welcomed and supported the idea of the meeting right from the outset.

The objectives of the Council of Europe, the spirit and the practical impact of its work, as well as its prestige, will undoubtedly encourage the participants to exchange information freely and work with a sense of togetherness.

From the outset our unanimous agreement with the principles of the Council of Europe has provided the basis for dialogue and personal and institutional acquaintance which gives us the opportunity, through the exchange of ideas and the sharing of feelings and experience, to build a future which the citizens of Europe have a right to expect.

We will be very satisfied if, at this extreme end of Europe, on this "strip of land bordered by the sea", to which we welcome you with gladness, affection and a will to communicate and co-operate, we are able to make a contribution, however small, to the achievement of the noble objectives for which we are all gathered here.

REQUIREMENTS FOR ADMISSION TO THE PROFESSIONS OF JUDGE AND PUBLIC PROSECUTOR - SELECTION CRITERIA AND MEANS OF RECRUITMENT

**Report presented by
Johann-Friedrich STAATS
Head of Department at the Federal Ministry of Justice**

Europeans are curious. They want to know how things are organised in other countries. Now this curiosity has even reached the judicial field. In Germany, at any rate, the training and status of judges and public prosecutors in other countries of Europe is almost *terra incognita*. I therefore wish to congratulate Portugal and the Council of Europe, and hope that this multilateral meeting will allow us to penetrate further into this unknown terrain and discover the riches of different judicial cultures in specific fields. Portugal, the country from which the voyages of discovery were launched, is a very apt venue. I wish to thank you for your kind invitation. It is a special experience to be here in Lisbon and take part in this meeting.

As I see it, the theme of this morning's session has two parts — firstly, the requirements for admission to the professions of judge and public prosecutor and, secondly, selection criteria and means of recruitment. I shall attempt to give you some idea of the situation in Germany, beginning with requirements for admission.

I first wish to point out that requirements for admission to the national legal service are, by law and in practice, identical for judges and public prosecutors. The German law on the status of judges and public prosecutors lays down three criteria on which admission is based. Candidates must:

- German nationality,

- have moral character such as to guarantee that the individual will uphold the free democratic constitutional system at all times, and

- be qualified to perform the duties of a judge (the technical term in German is *Befähigung zum Richteramt*).

This last criterion can only be met by those who have undergone long, demanding training. This is of course the usual obstacle to be overcome by anyone wishing to pursue a judicial career. Training takes place in two stages: university studies, ending with a first State examination, and in-service training, leading to a second State examination.

I.I would like to describe briefly the stages in the training of a German judge or prosecutor, or even of German legal specialists in general. After sitting exams at the age of 19 or 20, and in the case of young men after completing a period of military or civilian service, students enrol with one of the forty universities having law faculties. They attend lectures, take part in tutorials, do homework on legal subjects, sit tests and take an active role in study groups in order to increase their knowledge. The main objective of the university course is to develop an ability to solve concrete problems, such as those encountered in practice in the courts or in a barrister's chambers. By law legal studies must last at least three and a half years. However, on average students wait longer before registering to sit the first State examination (*erste juristische Staatsprüfung*), which ends the university course. The average student sits this examination after five years' studies (10.39 semesters in 1995). The first State examination lasts about six months and covers all the subjects dealt with at university. It involves written papers (*Klausuren*) supervised by invigilators. In the North German *Länder* students also have to submit a paper that they work on at home during a set period of four to six weeks. Students then have to sit orals. After this fairly demanding examination, which about one quarter of students fail at their first attempt, a "candidate" (there is no other word) who has passed the examination registers for two years of practical training (a traineeship), organised at the level of each *Land*. Almost all those who succeed in the examination move on to this form of in-service training. At this stage the young legal specialist becomes a probationary civil servant (whose appointment is not yet permanent) with the title of *Referendar* and receives a salary (currently about 2 000 Deutschmarks per month). This practical training consists of mandatory periods spent in the civil and criminal courts or the public prosecutor's office, in an administrative department or with a legal firm and ends with a traineeship of the candidate's choice within an appropriate body. On completing in-service training, the *Referendar* sits the second State examination (*zweite juristische Staatsprüfung*). This examination also lasts about six months and involves both supervised written papers (supplemented in the North German *Länder* with a paper written at home) and orals (an oral report on a case study and an interview with a panel). The examination covers all the subjects dealt with during in-service training, with special emphasis on procedural law and practical work. For instance, one paper consists in drafting a judgment or indictment. The second State examination is not considered easy either, although the failure rate is only in the region of 10 %. Successful candidates are awarded a certificate qualifying them to hold the office of judge for life. Despite its name, this certificate also allows admission to all the other legal professions existing in Germany, without any need, at least in theory, to undergo additional training.

II. This brings me to the second part: selection criteria and means of recruitment of German judges and prosecutors.

1. Judges and public prosecutors are recruited by the *Länder* rather than by a central institution. There is a large supply of jurists qualified to hold the office of judge or public prosecutor, which is considered an attractive job and is also fairly well paid at present, a possible further source of motivation.

2. An applicant for the office of judge or public prosecutors usually applies to the relevant *Land* minister immediately after sitting the second State examination. There is no competitive entry examination. The *Land* minister of justice is responsible for

selecting judges of the ordinary courts and often also the administrative and tax courts, while the *Land* minister for social affairs or labour is, in most cases, responsible for recruiting judges for the social security and labour courts.

3.   In most *Länder* the competent minister, usually the *Land* minister of justice, has sole discretion to decide on a recruitment.

In several *Länder* judges are recruited with the assistance of an Appointments Board. These boards are mainly made up of members of parliament or their representatives and members of the judiciary. There are also one or two lawyers. The minister cannot recruit anyone without a favourable decision from the Appointments Board.

On the whole the executive is in a strong position in this respect. Recruitment of judges through a competitive examination is regarded as unconstitutional in Germany.

4.   Article 33, paragraph 2 of the German Basic Law lays down the recruitment criteria, which are aptitude, qualification and professional achievement. Equal opportunity of access to the judiciary is thus guaranteed. This principle is binding on ministers and on the Appointments Board, where it is mandatory that such a Board should participate in the recruitment process. In practice the deciding factor is the examination results, especially the mark obtained in the second State examination. This explains why a competitive entry examination is not regarded as necessary. If there is some doubt, the marks obtained by the applicant during in-service training may also be taken into account. Some *Länder* provide for applicants to be interviewed. The importance placed on examination results involves a risk of recruiting applicants who, although they may be excellent jurists, are not suited to fulfil the duties of a judge. In this respect, the trial period constitutes a form of safety net. I will come back to this shortly.

5.   The recruitment process ends with an appointment. Appointment is a formal procedure. The applicant is given an official document, which must include the words "You are appointed as judge ...". The judge then takes the oath. However, taking the oath does not have any impact on the validity of the appointment.

6.   A newly recruited judge will be on probation for a period of no less than three years and no more than five years. This means that the judge can be dismissed from office during that period of time, should it transpire that he or she is not suited to the duties of a judge. A newly recruited judge may immediately carry out almost all judicial functions in the lower courts and receives the same salary as a judge with life tenure, but has not yet been assigned to a permanent post with a given court. *Inter alia*, such judges may be transferred to another court, a legal administrative department or a public prosecutor's office without their consent being required. Most judges appointed on probation successfully complete their trial period and are subsequently appointed permanently. However, it is not unusual for judges on probation to resign of their own initiative or be dismissed and to then follow another career, such as that of lawyer. As we have seen, such a change does not necessitate further training. A

person wanting to become a public prosecutor is appointed either as a probationary civil servant or a probationary judge. Some *Länder* have adopted the practice of making trainees spend their probationary period alternating between the duties of a judge and those of a public prosecutor. Once an individual has been appointed to the post of judge with life tenure or in the case of a public prosecutor (*Staatsanwalt*) as a permanent civil servant, switching between the two functions is rarer, although from a legal standpoint it remains possible at any time.

7. To a more limited extent, some judges are recruited as judges "under mandate". This path is open to public officials holding a permanent appointment or appointed for a specified duration who wish to pursue a career as a judge. Such transfers are, for example, more frequent between departments of the treasury and the tax courts. Like judges on probation, judges appointed under a mandate complete a trial period, but nevertheless have a fall-back solution in that they retain their rights as civil servants. If need be, they can always return to a civil service job.

8. Purely in order to give a full picture, it should be pointed out that in some *Länder* Appointments Boards are involved in the decision to give a probationer life tenure. In most cases there is no provision for such participation and it is the relevant minister, i.e. usually the *Land* minister of justice, who takes the decision alone.

The situation with regard to promotions is different. In many *Länder* provision is made for Appointments Boards to be involved in career management decisions. The Federal Appointments Board (comprising 16 *Land* ministers and 16 people appointed by the *Bundestag*, most of whom are members of parliament) is of particular importance. By agreement with the relevant federal minister, it selects those to be appointed as judges of the supreme federal courts.

9. At the Constitutional Court half of the judges are appointed by a parliamentary committee and the other half by the *Bundesrat* (the Federal Council representing the *Länder*).

SELECTION OF JUDGES

Report presented by
Ana Maria PÉREZ TÓRTOLA
Member of the Consejo General del Poder Judicial

It is recognised that one of the issues with regard to the selection of judges is the authority or body which is responsible for selection. There is a basic distinction between those cases where the selection is carried out by the State authority and those where judges are directly elected by the people, the so-called "popular Justice". With regard to the State authority's recruiting body a further distinction can be drawn whereby judges may be appointed either by the executive power (U.K.) or by the legislative power (for instance, the members of the German Constitutional Court), or by judges themselves (Italy), or finally, by bodies which are formed by members of various State powers.

A second significant feature is the fundamental difference existing between a so-called "technical Justice" (administered by professionals) and a "lay Justice" (administered by non-jurists, i.e. by individuals who are not necessarily legal experts).

The third criterion distinguishes between those systems where judges belong to a "judicial career" (using the Spanish term) and are employed as "civil servants", and, other systems where judges do not enjoy that status. When designing a legal system of recruitment these distinctions should be taken into account.

The competence of selection in Spain belongs to the General Council of Judiciary ("Consejo General del Poder Judicial"), whose membership and appointment system guarantees a significant degree of autonomy and self-government.

In my opinion, the choice of system determines the legal system for the selection of judges.

The Spanish legal system has three characteristics:

- a constitutional body that is in charge of the selection of judges.

- Spanish judges must be jurists (i.e. at least have a law degree) - except for the Justice of the Peace.

- Spanish judges are "civil servants" of some sort and this is a life-long employment.

It should also be noted that the constitutional body — the General Council of the Judiciary — has 20 members appointed by the Parliament and is considered to be the self-overning authority for the selection of judges.

Since our Constitution was adopted in 1978, there have been at least two models of the General Council of the Judiciary in Spain. The first one was criticized because of its rather "professionalist behaviour". Furthermore, it played a fairly "corporativist/ professionalist" part against the other State powers and institutions partly due to the way it was then elected even though its competency was extensive. In 1985, the appointment of the members of the Council of the Judiciary underwent a profound change and its competency was reduced. The power to select/recruit judges was then lost.

In the last few years, the General Council of the Judiciary has been claiming powers not only related to the "permanent training" of judges — a power it has always kept — but also to the selection/recruitment and initial training of judges - a power which until recently has belonged to the Ministry of Justice. It was argued that there was no reason for keeping both aspects separate, that they were intimately connected and that the initial and subsequent training of judges should follow similar guidelines.

In November 1994, a very important legal reform enabled the General Council of the Judiciary to assume the responsibility of selecting and initial training of judges. In accordance with the new legal text of the Judiciary Act, to become a judge requires an examination to be passed as a pre-condition to being admitted into the Judicial School — the judges' selection and training centre. This examination was intended to secure a certain degree of legal knowledge. A training period in this Judicial School is also envisaged.

The Judiciary Act also stresses the importance of this second phase.

For admittance into the Judicial School it is estimated that there are two possibilities:

1. To take a conventional exam it is necessary to have a law degree.

2. Another access system is provided for jurists who must accredit a previous professional experience of at least six years as lawyers, professors... They must go through an interview to assess not only their specific knowledge but also their professional experience.

Once at the Judicial School, there is a second period. The candidate-judges receive theoretical and practical training for a minimum period of two years. Generally speaking, the theoretical aspects which are to be instrumental in the judge's future work are taught at the selection and training centre, which depends directly on the General Council of the Judiciary. Practical training is to be achieved by making future judges work as assistants to professional judges who will control and assess the candidate's progress.

This new system is a challenge for the General Council of the Judiciary, and its results will be seen in the next years. Hard work is now being undertaken to prepare the statutory framework that will govern the selection and initial training of judges and the future of the Judicial School. This framework must be issued next month. We hope that this new legislation will be useful in improving the quality of justice and will help to provide a better administration of justice.

REQUIREMENTS FOR ADMISSION TO THE PROFESSIONS OF JUDGE AND PUBLIC PROSECUTOR - SELECTION CRITERIA AND MEANS OF RECRUITMENT

Report presented by
Fernando ESCRIBANO MORA
Secretary General, Ministry of Justice

The special characteristics of the Spanish system for recruiting judges and public prosecutors can be explained briefly by describing the differences in recruitment and initial training for these two professional categories.

It should be pointed out first of all that the procedures for recruiting judges have just been modified by Institutional Act 16/1994 of 8 November 1994. Under the act, overall responsibility for recruiting judges, which previously lay with the Ministry of Justice, has now been assigned by the Government and Parliament to the Judicial Service Commission. The transitional period is now coming to an end and the Ministry of Justice is currently carrying out a final selection of candidates before handing over responsibility to the Commission.

Although the reform was needed urgently and was called for by the Judicial Service Commission, it is still only partial. Reform of the recruitment of members of the State Prosecutor's Office will follow, but for the moment the Ministry of Justice is still responsible for their recruitment.

So, the first difference between judges and public prosecutors is that selection is carried out by different bodies. Nonetheless, the selection examinations which candidates for both professions are required to sit are virtually the same. Moreover, Article 42 of the regulations governing the State Prosecutor's Office stipulates that the system for recruiting prosecutors should be analogous to those for recruiting judges and that the same admission requirements should apply to both professions.

The second important difference concerns the admission procedures. There are two ways of becoming a member of the judiciary, which in Spain comprises three distinct functions: those of judge sitting alone (*juez*), judge sitting as part of a bench in higher courts (*magistrado*) and judge at the Court of Cassation. The first way is through a standard entry examination which is open to all candidates with a law degree and involves tests to evaluate their knowledge of the law. The second is a parallel method of recruitment, open to those who have been in legal practice for at least six years and which takes the form of an interview to assess the candidate's knowledge and experience.

The final difference between the professions of judge and public prosecutor lies in the initial training. Judges are trained by the Judicial Service Commission by way of a two-year course of study at the Judiciary School. The authority responsible for training public prosecutors is the Ministry of Justice. Until this year training lasted six months, but we are anxious to extend it to one or even one-and-a-half years. The training courses differ in content as well as duration. Both include periods of practical training, but judges receive this training in the courts while public prosecutors are trained in prosecutor's offices. Finally, whereas the training of future judges focuses mainly on civil and criminal law and procedure, that of public prosecutors concentrates primarily on criminal law and procedure and on matters which come within the ambit of the prosecution service in civil, administrative and social cases and cases involving minors.

THE FRENCH SYSTEM FOR RECRUITING JUDGES AND PUBLIC PROSECUTORS

**Report presented by
Daniel LUDET
Director of the Ecole Nationale de la Magistrature**

In France the "magistrature" is composed of both professional judges and members of the public prosecutor's department. Both are known as "magistrats".

In the French system all professional judges and public prosecutors are recruited according to the same rules.

I would now like to explain these rules to you.

There are two methods for recruiting judges and public prosecutors in France:

- recruitment by competitive entrance examination to the *Ecole nationale de la magistrature*;
- "direct" or "lateral" recruitment.

I.   Recruitment by competitive entrance examination for admission to the Ecole Nationale de la Magistrature

Students are admitted to the *Ecole nationale de la magistrature* by a competitive examination comprising anonymous written papers followed by oral tests. This competitive examination is not an open examination as the number of places is limited.

The candidates' merit is assessed by a board of examiners chaired by a judge of the Court of Cassation and including both ordinary and administrative court judges and professors of law.

For the time being there are in practice two types of competitive examination:

* **a competitive examination for students**, or "first competition", open to candidates up to the age of 27 who have a degree representing four years of university studies after the baccalauréat (A-levels); it should be noted that a degree in law is not expressly required;

* **a competitive examination for civil servants**, or "second competition", open to candidates up to the age of 40 who have completed at least four years' service in a government department; it should be noted that it is not necessary to have a degree to be allowed to sit this examination.

The **first competitive examination** is the one that offers the greatest number of posts (approximately 80 to 100) but both examinations are of the same standard and based on identical tests.

The tests concern general knowledge and either private or public law.

There is a considerable number of legal papers. Therefore, although the rules governing the competitive examinations do not require candidates to have degrees in law, their success in the examination presupposes that they have a high level of legal knowledge.

Some practical observations can be made concerning these examinations:

* as regards the first competitive examination, it has been noted that in the past few years requirements have become more and more stringent: in 1992 there were 8 candidates for 1 post, in 1993, 16 candidates for 1 post, in 1994, 18 candidates for 1 post (in the 1960s and 1970s there were only 3 to 5 candidates for each vacancy);

* still regarding the first examination, there is an ever-increasing number of female candidates: almost 7 candidates out of 10 are women and the same proportion is found amongst those who succeed; since the beginning of the 1980s most of the candidates admitted to the school have been women and it is now obvious that in a few years' time women will be in the majority in the judiciary, which now includes 47% of women;

* as regards the second competitive examination, there has been a relative decline in the number of candidates over the past few years in relation to the number of posts offered: there are scarcely more than 3 candidates for 1 post; this is a problem of standards as was illustrated in 1993 by the fact that the examining board did not fill all of the 20 posts offered and transferred 7 of these posts to the first competitive examination. The same happened in 1994.

A final remark: a State Authorities Act of February 1992 introduced a third type of competitive examination, open to persons who have 8 years' professional experience, or have held office as a local representative, or have exercised the functions of a lay judge. The decree implementing this law has not yet been passed. It should, however, be noted that this examination does not require candidates to have a degree either.

II. Direct recruitment to the judiciary

Anyone who has a degree representing four years of university studies after the *baccalauréat* and has professional experience which makes them particularly suitable for judicial duties can be a candidate for direct integration into the judiciary. The candidate must have practised for his or her profession for at least seven years in order to be integrated at the second level and at least 17 years to be integrated at the first level.

A candidate can only be directly appointed as a judge with the consent of a committee chaired by the First President of the Court of Cassation and mainly composed of elected judges.

The Ministry of Justice submits the applications to the committee, which may require a candidate to follow a probationary training period of six months at the most before giving its decision. An assessment is made at the end of this training period in court, which is organised by the *Ecole nationale de la magistrature*.

At the end of the training period, candidates are interviewed by the board responsible for grading legal trainees, which gives an opinion on their ability to perform judicial duties. The committee then gives its decision on the candidate's application.

If it gives a favourable opinion, it may decide that candidates should follow a specialised training course of up to six months before actually taking office.

In practice direct recruitment is not the main method for entering the judiciary, compared with the school's competitive entrance examinations. In some years, direct recruitment can account for up to 25 or 30% of total appointments if there are many vacant posts. At present scarcely more than 10% of posts are filled in this way. The candidates are usually lawyers or civil servants or, for the past few years, legal advisers from the private sector.

Conclusion

The competitive entrance examinations for admission to the *Ecole nationale de la magistrature* and direct recruitment are two completely different methods of being admitted to the judiciary. However, in either case an effort is made to apply objective criteria for selection, based on candidates' abilities and professional skills.

I would like to take a brief look at these selection criteria.

It would appear that recruitment by means of a competitive examination for admission to the *Ecole nationale de la magistrature* is based on rather abstract, formal or academic selection criteria. The number of legal papers is considerable even if the general knowledge papers and, in particular, the oral exam give the examining board some idea of candidates' personalities.

It is true that the French system emphasises objective selection criteria and does not, unlike the systems in other countries, make use of psychological tests.

However, it should be said that training at the *Ecole nationale de la magistrature* is of a probationary type. During the 31 months spent at the school, students' aptitude is assessed, particularly during a one-year practical training course in a court. At the end of the school period the examining board responsible for grading the students bases its decision as to whether the students are fit to become judges on these assessments.

This means that the students' psychological qualities are not assessed as such, ie in abstract terms, but rather in practical terms by judging candidates' conduct on the job. Consequently this assessment of candidates is - and we consider this essential - entirely objective.

A similar remark can be made concerning direct recruitment in that in practice it is the candidates' trial period in a court which is decisive for the assessment of their capabilities and therefore determines whether they will become judges.

REQUIREMENTS FOR ADMISSION TO THE PROFESSIONS OF JUDGE AND PUBLIC PROSECUTOR - SELECTION CRITERIA AND MEANS OF RECRUITMENT

Report presented by
Joep J.I. VERBURG
Principal of the Stichting Studiecentrum Rechtspleging

The judiciary in the Netherlands consists of about 1600 judges and 400 public prosecutors for a population of about 15 million people.

This judiciary is divided into two branches.

On the one hand there are regular or ordinary courts with jurisdiction in criminal and civil (family and commercial) cases, and on the other hand there is a more complex system of administrative tribunals.

There is currently a total review of the judicial organisation which will lead to the merger of the various administrative tribunals with the system of regular courts. Justice has to be done in two or three instances; civil and criminal matters, as a rule, in three instances and administrative disputes, as a rule, in two instances.

Judges and public prosecutors are considered to be members of the judiciary or, as we also call it, the magistrature. It is also recognised that the public prosecutor has a special position. There is a certain hierarchy which enables senior staff up to the Minister of Justice to give instructions to junior staff regarding detection and prosecution of punishable acts. (The public prosecutor's department at the Supreme Court is not included in this hierarchy).

In contrast to judges, public prosecutors have the same legal status as ordinary civil servants. When they are incompetent or when they function badly, action such as dismissal and transfer by the Minister of Justice are, in principle, possible.

Despite this special position, members of the Crown are traditionally considered members of the judiciary, because:

- they have the legal task of the enforcement of justice,

- they exercise judicial powers, and

- they are not tied up in court by general instructions if the trial gives cause for a divergent point of view.

This point of view is primary in recruitment, selection and professional training.

For some time now the policy concerning the composition of the judiciary in the Netherlands has been: 50% young jurists as inside trainees and 50% experienced jurists from outside. This safeguards against inbreeding. It is considered very important to have a mix of people with different experience.

The formal requirements for new trainees requires them to be under 30 years of age, of good behaviour, Dutch nationality, and holding a Dutch law degree. The Ministry of Justice indicates at each recruitment period how many trainees can be admitted. In the last 4 years 25 trainees have been admitted in each year during the months of April, and the same number in October.

About 450 candidates apply. The selection procedure lasts about 7 months and is finalised 3 months before the starting date of the new curriculum.

Selection starts with an intelligence test carried out by external consultants (this is currently the former state psychology office). In this first test the general abilities and general intelligence of the candidate are assessed.

A number of candidates drop out, the best go on to the next test. This is a group of about 100 people. These people have to complete a second psychology test which is a personality test. Following this, all candidates have to appear before the selection committee. The committee is composed of three members of the judiciary, one representative of the Minister of Justice and one outsider. The outsider represents society. This person could, for example, be a journalist, a member of the Bar, or a university professor. The committee forms an opinion about every candidate and later compares this opinion with the results of the psychology test. The result of the pscyhology test only has any influence when the committee has reservations about a candidate.

After this comparison the final decision is made. To arrive at a decision the members of the committee give every candidate points ranging from 2 to 9 for:

- motivation,
- examination results in the study of law,
- juridical qualities,
- social concern,
- good fellowship,
- working attitude,
- well-balanced,
- personal development.

The maximum number of points is 360 and a minimum of 270 points is necessary. By considering all of these aspects, the committee tries to be as objective as possible and to regulate the subjectivity of the members of the committee. The examination is competitive but the experience of many years has shown that successful candidates achieve 300 points or more.

The committee recommends to the Minister of Justice the 25 candidates with the highest number of points. The Minister of Justice will appoint the recommended candidates. In recent years about 75% of appointed candidates have been female. The group that started earlier this month was composed of a ratio of 20 females to every 5 males.

Requirements for outside jurists who wish to apply for nomination as a judge or public prosecutor are:

- a university degree in Dutch law,

- at least 6 years juridical experience (e.g. at the Bar, as a company lawyer, at a university or government post)

- Dutch nationality,

- good behaviour,

- not more than 50 years of age,

- good fellowship.

There is a specific committee of selection for outside jurists but we are preparing a new structure of only one committee divided into sections is now being created.

This method of selection is not competitive. After selection by the general committee the candidate is free to find a training position in one of the courts to become a judge. Normally the candidate knows beforehand about his chances of being admitted to the court of his preference. The placement of an incoming public prosecutor is more centralised as it is a responsibility shared between the Ministry of Justice and the local Public Prosecutor's office.

CONDITIONS OF ACCESS TO THE PROFESSION OF JUDGE AND PUBLIC PROSECUTOR

Report presented by
Armando LEANDRO
Director of the Centro de Estudos Judiciáros

In Portugal the requirements for access to the office of judge or public prosecutor are as follows:

- to be a Portuguese citizen;

- to enjoy full civic and civil rights;

- to be in possession of a master's degree in law obtained from a Portuguese university or recognised as an equivalent qualification in Portugal;

- to have attended and achieved favourable results in the courses of the *Centro de Estudos Judiciáros*, in accordance with the conditions laid down in the institutional act governing the centre;

- to satisfy the conditions laid down in the law on the appointment of civil servants.

In order to exercise the functions of a judge or public prosecutor therefore, it is necessary to have been admitted to the *Centro de Estudos Judiciáros* and successfully completed the initial training course which lasts for a total of 28 months and includes 10 months of theoretical and practical training, a 10 month induction course and 8 months training prior to receiving a post.

Each year the number of posts offered for competition depends on the instructions given to the Ministry of Justice by the Judicial Service Commission and the Commission of the Prosecuting Authorities.

To enter the *Centro de Estudos Judiciáros*, candidates must be at least 23 years of age at the beginning of the selection process and pass certain aptitude tests; doctors of law are not required to take the tests.

The tests are made up of two stages, one written and one oral.

However the following candidates are exempt from the written stage:

- barristers with at least seven years of professional experience who have received a favourable assessment from the bar;

- registrars and notaries with at least seven years of experience, who have been assessed as "good";

- clerks of court and law graduates in service for ten years, who have been assessed as "very good".

The number of candidates exempted from the written stage may not exceed 1/5 of the number of posts offered for competition.

The written stage comprises:

- an essay on a social, economic or cultural theme. During this test candidates may not refer to any texts or notes;

- solving a practical case of civil or commercial law or civil procedure;

- solving a practical case of criminal law or criminal procedure.

In the event of obvious inaptitude the written test is eliminatory.

The oral stage comprises:

- a conversation on legal, ethical and cultural aspects of themes which are announced in advance, for example, human rights, the ethical, organisational, functional and statutory aspects of the administration of justice as well as its features connected with inter-personal contact and social communication, methods of implementing the law, changes in society relating to the law, and new types of tasks for the legal system;

- a discussion on the written papers in civil and criminal law;

- an oral test on certain legal themes drawn by lot 48 hours before the test.

Examples of possible themes are constitutional law, administrative law, Community law, labour law, family and children's law, and various topics relating to the protection of the environment, consumer rights and cultural heritage.

The aptitude tests are held before examining boards made up of:

- judges appointed by the Judicial Service Commission;

- public prosecutors appointed by the Commission of the Prosecuting Authorities;

- the directors and teachers of the *Centro de Estudos Judiciáros* as well as individuals renowned for their knowledge and skill in the cultural field appointed by the Minister of Justice on the recommendation of the Director of the *Centro de Estudos Judiciáros*.

At the end of the tests candidates are divided into those who have passed and those who have failed. Successful candidates are given marks on a scale from 10 to 20.

The main aim is to train judges to be independent, responsible, reliable, technically competent and to have a sense of humility and duty as well as a mind which is open to culture and to life itself.

The intention is for would-be judges to be:

- careful and thorough in their observation, so that they can get behind external appearances;

- cautious and tolerant in their judgement so as to reduce the risk of making unjustified conclusions about individuals;

- thorough in their arguments and the justification of their decisions so that a sense of what is reasonable is reconciled as closely as possible with the applicable rule of the law as part of a non-absolutist concept of justice;

- aware of the relativity of human individuals, human life and the whole justice system;

- imaginative and responsible in the judgment of each specific case, so as to reconcile as far as possible justice and security.

These objectives are present right from the beginning of the training period and even form part of the selection process and criteria.

Therefore, as well as evaluating technical knowledge, efforts are made to assess, as much as possible, candidates' ethical and social attitudes, their intellectual capacity, their legal and general knowledge, their knowledge of the Portuguese language, and their ability to understand problems, to analyse, summarise, weigh up, reason, argue and come to decisions.

The training period is reserved for the development and assessment of general and specific skills relating to the performance of the judge's duties.

CONDITIONS OF ACCESS TO THE PROFESSION OF JUDGE AND PUBLIC PROSECUTOR - SELECTION CRITERIA AND RECRUITING PROCEDURES IN THE UNITED KINGDOM

Report presented by
Ian Campbell
Judge at the Queen Elizabeth II Law Courts at Liverpool

This text has been prepared as the written version of the oral report delivered by Judge Campbell at Lisbon on 27 April 1995. This written version does not in fact follow, nor does it seek to follow, word for word the oral report which was in the end delivered in English from notes earlier prepared with a view to speaking in French.

The United Kingdom is a unitary state which contains however three quite separate legal systems. These are those of England and Wales, Scotland and Northern Ireland. Whereas the system of Northern Ireland resembles in many ways that of England and Wales, the Scottish system is distinct. It developed as the system prevailing in the Kingdom of Scotland and was preserved by the Treaty of Union between the Kingdoms of England and Scotland, adopted by the countries' respective Parliaments in 1707. Historically the Scottish legal system may be regarded as having developed broadly along lines similar to the legal systems of many European countries. European influences were on the other hand of relatively little real importance in the evolution of the "common law" of England and Wales. Since the Union of the Parliaments in 1707 the legal systems of England and Wales and of Scotland have remained separate although each has no doubt, in various ways, influenced the other. The fact that the legal systems of England and Wales and of Scotland have remained separate since the Union of 1707 is perhaps a matter which gives food for thought and merits study within the context of the consideration of legal developments within the European Union today.

This report is essentially concerned with the legal system of England and Wales. It should be noted however that the various authorities concerned with the legal systems both of Scotland and Northern Ireland have kindly supplied material for distribution among the participants at this conference. Such material will enable those attending this meeting to take away and read at their leisure details concerning the Scottish and Northern Irish legal systems. The authorities of England and Wales too have been equally generous. Much source material is thus available to complement this short report.

It may be surprising to those who come from countries where the judges are, in general, professional judges, to find that in England and Wales 95% of the criminal work of the courts is carried out by non-professional judges, namely the magistrates for "Justices of the Peace" as they are also referred to, who sit part-time. There are about 30,000 Magistrates in England and Wales and the office of Justice of the Peace was created in the 14th century. One may find references to Justice of the Peace in English literature throughout the ages. Thus one of Chaucer's pilgrims heading for Canterbury in *The Canterbury Tales* was a Justice and likewise one may find a Justice in the works of Shakespeare representing one of the "seven ages of man". Justices of the Peace are appointed from all walks of life and the majority will probably be appointed when aged in their 30s, 40s or 50s. To become a Justice of the Peace is not to take a first step up a judicial "ladder". There is no promotion save to the extent that after training, and with the requisite seniority, a magistrate may be permitted to take the chair at a court sitting. (Ordinarily a chairman will sit with two Justices). Prior legal knowledge is not necessary nor even usual. As far as points of law arising at a hearing are concerned, magistrates are assisted by a legally trained court clerk. However, in recent years Justices have in fact been required to undergo some training. In all parts of England and Wales except the Duchy of Lancaster, Justices are appointed by the Lord Chancellor upon the advice of local advisory committees. Justices within the jurisdiction of the Duchy of Lancaster are appointed by the Chancellor of the Duchy of Lancaster albeit upon the same basis as those for the rest of England and Wales. In making appointments not only is an attempt made to appoint men and women from all walks of life but equally to obtain a bench of magistrates reflecting the balance of the political parties. It may be surprising to those not familiar with the system in England and Wales but it is a fact that the application form which a prospective magistrate is required to complete enquiries as to whether the applicant votes at general elections and, if so, for what party. It is however made entirely clear that support for one or other political party is in no sense a disqualification for appointment as a Justice. The information is sought simply so as to enable the Lord Chancellor and the advisory committee concerned with selection, to maintain a balanced bench.

The so-called stipendiary magistrates of whom there are approximately 100 in England and Wales exercise the same jurisdiction as the non-professional magistrates but they sit on their own and are professionally trained as barristers or solicitors. They are appointed by the Queen. Posts are advertised and there may be a number of applicants who will be interviewed and a selection made following upon such interviews. The minimum qualification to be appointed as stipendiary magistrate is to have had rights of audience in courts of the appropriate level for 7 years.

Magistrates have areas of jurisdiction in addition to crime including children's cases. District judges are paid at the same level as stipendiary magistrates but have jurisdiction in family and/or civil matters. Very recently the posts of district judge and the higher office of circuit judge have been advertised. District judges are appointed by the Lord Chancellor but circuit judges are appointed by the Queen upon the recommendation of the Lord Chancellor.

A full-time district judge will not normally be appointed before the age of 40 (nor after the age of 60), although he/she may well have begun sitting part-time in his/her 30s. The position of district judge is open to barristers or solicitors who have held rights of audience in courts of the appropriate level for a period of 7 years and who have sat for at least 2 years as a deputy district judge. Nowadays the deputy district judge (of whom there are about 750), or the Assistant Recorder or Recorder (of whom there are about 1,250), and who are part-time judges at the district judge level and the circuit judge level respectively, are seen as individuals who have taken the first step up the judicial ladder. Likewise the path of promotion is open for the stipendiary magistrate who may become a circuit judge. Circuit judges collectively have jurisdiction (subject to individual specialisation), in civil and family law matters as well as in crime. A full-time circuit judge will not normally be appointed before the age of 45 (nor after the age of 60), although he/she will have been sitting part- time for about a month a year as an assistant recorder (of whom there are over 400) from his/her late 30s and then for a similar period as a recorder (of whom there are over 800). The position is open to barristers and solicitors who have held rights of audience for a period of 10 years. There are about 8,000 barristers in England and Wales today and about 60,000 solicitors. In England and Wales there are approximately 312 full-time district judges and 514 circuit judges.

There are 98 High Court judges. Appointment as a High Court judge carries with it a Knighthood. The post is not open to application but solely offered by invitation. Until recent times the position was open to barristers only but it is now open to solicitors by way of promotion from the circuit bench. Recently the first such appointment has been made. The statutory qualification for appointment is to have held rights of audience in the High Court for 10 years or to have been a circuit judge for at least 2 years. Traditionally the post of High Court judge was filled from amongst those senior barristers who had "taken silk" and thus become Queen's Counsel.

The Lord Chancellor's Department maintains confidential dossiers concerning all applicants for judicial appointment. Such dossiers will have been compiled over a period and will include notes derived confidential consultations between a high official of the Lord Chancellor's Department and members of the judiciary. Nowadays applicants both for part-time and full-time judicial posts are interviewed. Thus a short-listed applicant for the post of circuit or district judge will be interviewed in each case by a panel of three, albeit differently composed, depending upon the level of post sought. In 1994 some controversy was caused when the Lord Chancellor indicated that he had agreed to lift the ban on civil servants who work as lawyers in the Government legal service being eligible for appointment as judges.

As far as "Public Prosecutors" are concerned it should in the first instance be appreciated that as far as England and Wales is concerned the prosecution of criminal proceedings is normally brought by the Crown Prosecution Service (CPS) which was set up in 1986. Its head is the Director of Public Prosecutions (DPP) who is "superintended" by and responsible to the Government's chief legal adviser, the Attorney General. The CPS is staffed by over 2,000 lawyers who are either barristers or solicitors but they would not be known as "public prosecutors". The CPS has a limited number of opportunities for trainee solicitors and pupil barristers each year. Recruitment of lawyers to the CPS is pursuant to advertisement and as the CPS has its own career structure entry opportunities exist at more than one level of professional experience for barristers or solicitors.

Serious fraud cases are prosecuted by the Serious Fraud Office (SFO) and there are certain other Government bodies such as the Inland Revenue, Department of Trade and Industry and Customs and Excise which prosecute cases arising out of their fields of responsibility. Once again legal staff are recruited from the ranks of barristers and solicitors but in these instances recruitment is carried out pursuant to advertisement by the Government Legal Service.

A private individual may launch a prosecution although this is something of a rarity. Very unusually this month a private prosecution for murder has in fact been commenced. The Attorney General has the power to take over such a prosecution himself and pursue it, or end it.

In the Crown Court the present situation is that the employees of the CPS and other Government bodies do not have the right of audience although the position in this respect is under constant review and may well shortly change. As matters presently stand the CPS or other prosecuting authority must instruct a barrister or solicitor who has such right of audience, normally a barrister although solicitors are fast acquiring equal rights.

Perhaps one may add this comment as to training, namely that there is a certain hesitation among a number of judges in England and Wales with regard to this topic. In view of its sensitivity the body which has the responsibility for training judges is in fact called the Judicial Studies Board. The reason for this sensitivity arises perhaps out of reasons of history. The legal system of England and Wales is one in which the "common law" has developed over the centuries essentially as judge-made law. If a student wished to know what the law was he would traditionally learn it from the judges. The academic study of law in England and Wales is in comparison with the situation prevailing elsewhere in Europe of relatively recent origin.[1] Nowadays however the scope for the development of "judge-made law" is greatly restricted. To take but one field the judges of England and Wales recognise of course the supremacy of European Law. It may well be therefore that in the context of the legal system of England and Wales, training will increase as time goes by. It is however interesting to note that insofar as assessment takes place within the context of training, it is the "trainers" and not the trainees who are assessed and evaluated.

Finally, and bearing in mind the multi-racial nature of British society, it should also be observed that all full and part-time circuit and district judges in England and Wales have participated in, or are about to participate in, residential seminars devoted exclusively to the study of ethnic issues.

---

[1] See R.C. Van Caenegen, *Judges, Legislators and Professors, Chapters in European Legal History* (Cambridge: University Press, 1987).

CONDITIONS OF ACCESS TO THE PROFESSION OF JUDGE AND PUBLIC PROSECUTOR (PROCURATOR) IN POLAND - SELECTION CRITERIA AND RECRUITING PROCEDURES

**Report presented by
Stanislaw WALTOŚ
Professor of Law, Universytet Jagellionski**

I.   The reasonable starting point for a discussion concerning the system of selection criteria and conditions for access to the profession of judges and public prosecution always seems to be the system of university education.

The average age of the first year student of law in Poland is about 19. Prior to university, students will have completed 8 years of grammar school education and 4 years spent in a high school. Polish law school programmes take five years to be completed for two models, i.e. for full time students and for part-time or extra-mural students. The curriculum is fairly theoretical in all schools of law. During the first year courses on legal history, history of systems of government and Roman law are prevalent. Such subjects represent about 40 % of the curriculum. During the next four years students attend lectures, seminars and classes on different branches of law taught mainly from a theoretical point of view. Students of course receive information on current reform movements, on important judicial decisions which have an impact on the judiciary, but this does not change the curriculum model. Students do not get any training in the practice of law. The case method is not broadly accepted and rooted in law schools in Poland. Likewise, the students get little practical instruction on how to formulate legal writs, how to conduct themselves during a trial, how to compute tax reductions, etc. According to an opinion common to university teachers, law schools should focus on the theory of law, rules and norms of law in force, the history and the present implementation of the norms. Practical aspects of law in action are believed to be beyond the scope of the instruction. There exists a presumption that graduates will have an opportunity to learn all "secrets" of law practice later, after they have graduated. In other words, law schools in Poland, like in many other countries which belong to the family of civil law, leave the instruction in practical implementation of theoretical knowledge to the practising lawyers on whose experience the graduates will rely. The majority of graduates are not older than 24-25. This means that their life experience is fairly limited. Before 1989, this experience was based rather on facts of students life and it did not abound in defeats or bitter losses which mark the decision making process. From 1989 on the situation has slightly changed. There are some law students who have engaged in small business and sometimes they have made money, not always by legitimate means. Nevertheless, such phenomena do not change the general situation characterised by the need to instruct graduates in the practice of law after they have completed their studies in the school of law.

II.   In Poland, there are two ways of becoming a judge and public prosecutor. The first way is for experienced lawyers, that is for advocates, notaries and legal advisers, who may enter the two professions provided that they have at least three years experience in their own professions or as University professors of law. It was only at the very beginning of the postcommunist era that several advocates and legal advisers took advantage of this possibility and entered the professions of judge or public prosecutor. Recently such cases have been very rare. As a result, in our discussion this way will not be considered.

The basic method of starting the career of judge or public prosecutor is to serve an apprenticeship that is known in Poland as "aplikacja". In this context it is however worthwhile to note that there exists no general Bar or State (like in Germany) examination that would allow a successful candidate to enter into all legal professions in Poland. Each legal profession formulates its own separate apprenticeship programme and both entry and final examinations are administered within the framework of this apprenticeship.

There are the following apprenticeship programmes in Poland: for judges, public prosecutors (procurators), advocates, legal advisers, notaries and public administration officers.

According to the Organisation of the Courts Act the objective of judicial apprenticeship is to provide the future judge with the knowledge of his functions and of court offices as well as to introduce him to the skills enabling him to perform the duties of his profession. The number of judge apprentices in Poland in recent years is shown below:

Year	Number
1989 -	664
1990 -	887
1991 -	992
1992 -	976
1993 -	809
1994 -	850

It is worthwhile to note that about 1/3 of all apprentices are unpaid and do their work voluntarily.

Public prosecution apprenticeship is aimed at preparing candidates to become public prosecutors (section 90 of the Public Prosecutor Office Act of 1986 with amendments, Journal of Law 1993, No.19, pos.70, am, year 1994, No. 105, pos. 509). The number of public prosecutor apprentices in Poland in recent years is shown below:

Year	Number
1989 -	536
1990 -	356
1991 -	256
1992 -	290
1993 -	340
1994 -	512

While comparing the total number of all graduates from law schools in Poland in 1992 (3 355) with the total number of apprentices in courts and public prosecutor offices in the year 1993 (809 + 340 = 1 149), we may reach the conclusion that only about 1/3 of all graduates successfully enter the judicial apprenticeships. The remainder apply for the advocates, notaries, administrative or legal advisers apprenticeships.

Why do we have separate apprenticeships for judges and public prosecutors?

The explanation of a such situation lies in historical circumstances. Until 1950 public prosecution departments and courts were, like in France, subordinated to the Minister of Justice who in addition performed the function of the Chief Public Prosecutor. With the sovietisation of the Polish legal system in 1950 courts were separated from public prosecution offices. An independent structure of procuratura (public prosecution) was established, which was formally subordinated to the Head of State. Consequently, apprenticeships were divided into two. In 1990, procuratura or public prosecution was included into the structure of the Ministry of Justice, who once again became the Chief Public Prosecutor. Despite this reform, the tradition of separate apprenticeships survived.

However the Ordinance of the Minister of Justice of 8 September 1993, Journal of Law. No.109, pos.491) already provides for joint regulation pertaining to the duties and privileges of apprentices of both types, their examinations and exemptions from examinations. Nevertheless the Ordinance does not do away with separate judicial and public prosecutor apprenticeships. Judicial and public prosecutor final examinations that are held upon the completion of the two apprenticeships are also separate (§ 26 and 39). As a result of separate apprenticeships being maintained, the future judge is not sufficiently instructed in criminalistics, forensic medicine, forensic psychiatry and psychology. Also his knowledge of administrative law and its procedures is limited. The potential public prosecutor in turn is not obliged to demonstrate thorough knowledge of economic law, labour law and social security.

III. Each apprenticeship has its own program. Its authors formulated it having in view exclusively the profession for which the specific apprenticeship is a preparation. They therefore tried to make the objectives of the specific apprenticeship fit the requirement of the appropriate legal profession and ignored the possible shifts of future lawyer from one legal profession to another.

The law graduate who has selected the career of judge or public prosecutor has to pass at least two exams before being nominated. The first one is the entry exam that allows him to enter apprenticeship. The second one is the final exam that allows him to become a judge or a public prosecutor.

Certainly the broadest program is that of the advocate apprenticeship. Upon the final exam, the advocate (lawyer) apprentices must answer questions concerning civil law and its procedures, family law, labour law and the law on social security, administrative law and its procedures, law on advocacy, the lawyers' code of ethics and administration of justice (§ 38 of Regulation on Advocacy Apprenticeship).

It is worthwhile to note that when the candidate applies to be enrolled in the list of apprentices the submission of his diploma is a purely formal requirement. In fact the submission is required only after the given individual has already been recruited. This is so because the recruitment for both judicial and public prosecution apprenticeships always begins before the academic year has been completed which means that the recruitment starts before the Magister (British L.L.B) exams are taken. It is also as early as May each year that the entry exams for judicial apprenticeship are announced and therefore for that reason the submission of the Magister diploma cannot be required. The same is true about the entry exam for public prosecution. The grades obtained during studies, the topic of Magister thesis as well as the appraisal of the thesis in most cases have no effect on the decision as to whether or not the graduate will be enrolled in the judicial apprenticeship. They do not have any effect on the candidate's successful entering the public prosecutor or any other apprenticeship either.

The entry exams are called competitions for apprenticeships or qualification procedures and and are - as a rule - organised without the University representatives participating in them. In fact the law (§ 12 sect.1 and § 35 sect.1 of the previously mentioned Ordinance of the Minister of Justice of 1993) provides for the possibility for members of the University teaching staff to attend the entry exams for judicial and public prosecution apprenticeships. That does not mean however that the University teachers really do attend them.

IV. The lack of interchangeability is the cause of considerable complications in the life of a young lawyer who, upon completing his apprenticeship, may be determined to change his profession in law. If for instance a judicial apprentice who has successfully passed his final judicial exam is applying for the advocate apprenticeship he, if accepted, would have to meet two additional requirements, i.e. he would have to prolong his apprenticeship by two additional years (unlike judicial apprenticeship, the advocate apprenticeship lasts for 4 and not 2 years) and at its end he would have to successfully pass the advocate exam.

Let us take for a change a public prosecutor apprentice who, having successfully passed the public prosecutor exam, applies to the court for an appointment as a judge. The skills he has acquired allow him to know how to conduct himself in a public prosecution and not how to conduct himself in the court. This will not facilitate his work as an assistant judge if he is nominated to be one.

V. In late 1960s the existing training centre for public prosecutors in Warsaw was closed. As early as the late 1950s a similar training centre for judges in Jozefowo was closed. I am fully convinced that it would be necessary to rethink the problem of reopening such professional centres.

The reform of education in law would appear to be urgent. It should start with practising lawyers who are responsible for organizing apprentplaceiceships respecting University diplomas. The grades obtained during University studies should be factually and not only formally taken into consideration. In the course of law studies more emphasis should be placed on the practice of law although drastic changes are unadvisable in this respect. The University is undoubtedly primarily responsible for teaching theory. This does not mean however that the University teacher whose courses have strict links with practice should ignore the discussion of the ways in which the law is in practice implemented. On the contrary, it seems that the case study method, if applied within reasonable boundaries, might help students acquire the skills required for classifying and analysing factual events within the scope of legal norms.

It is also high time that the unification of apprenticeships was seriously debated. A joint apprenticeship organised for those applying for the profession of judge, public prosecutor, legal adviser, advocate and notary would seem advisable.

Such an apprenticeship should take 3 years to be completed. While completing it, the apprentices might have to take a final exam, the successful passing of which would allow them to perform any of the aforementioned legal professions. Changing from one profession to another would be facilitated. Having completed such an apprenticeship, a young jurist would have a better chance of finding a job that would really suit him. Also employers would have a larger group of candidates from amongst whom to select the right employee.

There is one more suggestion that needs to be discussed. I believe that one of the most important changes to be enacted would be the formulation of the new conditions of promotion to the profession of a judge and of a public prosecutor. I am deeply convinced that young lawyers should have at least two years practical experience in their professional career before being promoted to the profession of judge or public prosecutor (procurator). This would guarantee that they possess a certain life experience which is indispensable for everybody who performs the duties of judge or public prosecutor.

THE INITIAL TRAINING OF JUDGES : THE FRENCH EXPERIENCE

Report presented by
Maud VIGNAU
Director of Initial Training
at the Ecole Nationale de la Magistrature

The *Ecole Nationale de la Magistrature* (ENM) was established in 1958 for the purpose of improving recruitment, guaranteeing the professional skills of judges and enhancing the status of the judiciary.

Over a period of 35 years the *Ecole Nationale de la Magistrature* - the only institution for training judges in France - trained 5,500 of the 6,300 judges now in office.

In order to facilitate comparisons, I would like to remind you briefly of the two main characteristics of the French judicial system: Courts dealing with administrative disputes are completely separate from other courts - I will confine my observations to methods of recruiting and training judges for ordinary courts. The French judiciary brings together, within a single body, judges and representatives of the public prosecutor's department - judges and public prosecutors have a career and they may change functions several times during their working life ie. they may alternate between the functions of judge and public prosecutor.

Candidates who pass one of the competitive examinations are appointed legal trainees. They take the oath in a Court of Appeal and become members of the *Ecole Nationale de la Magistrature* for a training period lasting 31 months.

The number of students varies from one year to the next, depending on the number of vacancies which the Ministry of Justice makes available for those who pass the examination.

As soon as they take up their studies at the ENM the students are paid by the State (approximately FRF 9,500 per month - $1,900/2,000).

The initial training of judges

The training given by the ENM is a professional training designed to turn a legal expert into a judge capable of carrying out all the functions of a judge or public prosecutor.

Students are already considered to have the necessary legal knowledge if they pass the entrance examination. The initial training is therefore intended to encourage the acquisition of skills and to encourage students to develop their personal qualities.

Consequently the aims of the course are as follows:

- to provide students with methodology and a high level of professional know-how, designed to ensure that justice is reliably administered;

- to make them aware of and able to analyse the human, economic and social environment of the law;

- to encourage students to analyse judicial functions, the basic principles of judges' action, their status and ethics.

I. The acquisition of professional skills

The professional skills of judges are an essential safeguard for defendants: they ensure not only legal security but also procedural security and the safeguarding of individual freedom.

The *Ecole nationale de la magistrature* does not really provide legal training in the form of law classes. Legal trainees are considered to have already acquired sufficient education and knowledge during their university studies.

The stringent criteria applied in admitting students to the ENM ensures that only the best students become members of the judiciary.

The ENM provides two forms of training in techniques and skills peripheral to the legal field.

The former involves the study of the different functions exercised by specialised judges and public prosecutors using practical examples and as far as possible actual case files.

The latter concerns fields as varied as forensic medicine, psychology, psychiatry and interview, communication and data-processing techniques.

In addition to the acquisition of technical skills, the objective is to study the environment in which the courts operate.

II. Being aware of and being able to analyse the human, economic and social environment of the law

The *Ecole nationale de la magistrature* takes pains to allow legal trainees to discover the environment in which they will work once they become judges.

Through training courses outside the judicial establishment, they gradually become acquainted with other professions with which judges have to work: lawyers, social workers, police officers, the constabulary, the authorities and experts.

By participating in enquiries, legal trainees are required to analyse events prior to and following court action, to understand the demands made by the law and to assess the impact of their decisions.

From a more general point of view, trainees take advantage of the time spent in the ENM to become acquainted with the most important contemporary issues.

III. Analysing judicial functions

The main aim of the training is to enable future judges to acquire a "professional level of legal culture".

The acquisition of this culture entails a deep understanding of the role of a judge and an exact knowledge of the basic principles and ethical rules.

The acquisition of a professional level of legal culture presupposes a knowledge of subjects other than law, for instance sociology, history, philosophy and psychology.

The initial training period

The training period lasts 31 months and is divided into two separate stages:

A general multi-disciplinary stage lasting 25 months (this aspect of the training is necessitated by the way in which the courts are organised and the status of judges).

It includes a three-month training course outside the French judiciary, which takes place in companies, government departments or foreign courts. Legal trainees must participate actively and be placed in a position of responsibility in the host institution.

After this part of the training there is a seven-month study period at the school in Bordeaux.

This period is devoted to providing legal trainees with all the professional know-how they will need in terms of both legal techniques and relationships with those with whom they will work as judges; it should also encourage trainees to give thought to the exercise of judicial functions. The study period in Bordeaux is devoted to tuition in the form of lectures and tutorials.

The teaching is not normally of an academic or university type but should be more practical.

The school has a permanent teaching staff of 17 lecturers who are judges released from their normal duties for several years; however the school also calls on the services of 150 other specialists in the most varied subjects: law, history, sociology, psychology, psychiatry, forensic medicine, accounting etc.

Although the training is based mainly on practice, considerable importance is also attached to reflection and judicial practices are often subject to criticism.

At the end of this period a 14-month training course in a court enables trainees to carry out each of the main judicial functions (trainees are placed in practical situations, they have to draft decisions and preside over proceedings). During the training course in courts, legal trainees are initiated in the actual practice of different judicial functions under the supervision of and with the advice of judges of that particular court. Students actually carry out the functions of judges and public prosecutors but their signature alone on the various decisions is not sufficient.

During the training period in court they also take part in other placements: for example they may choose to be warders, tutors or deputy governors in prisons, to work in a police station or constabulary, in a bailiff's office or in a lawyer's practice. During this final two-month training period, legal trainees are introduced to the work of the Bar as if they were barristers and may therefore have to defend a case before a court.

At the end of this first stage of general training trainees have to take a final exam to assess their aptitude to exercise judicial functions and to establish their grade. Their abilities are therefore monitored (a trainee may be excluded from the course or requested to repeat that part of the course), which means that the training provided by the ENM is a probational form of training.

After having chosen, in accordance with their grade, a position from a list submitted by the Ministry of Justice, trainees begin the second and final part of their training.

This second 'specialised' stage, lasts five months. The training, which is both theoretical and practical, focuses on preparing students for their first post. These first posts are usually as judges in regional courts or judges in courts of first instance, investigating judges, judges dealing with children, judges responsible for the execution of sentences, deputy public prosecutors or public prosecutors. At the end of this specialisation, students are appointed to the courts to which they have been assigned by a decree issued by the President of the Republic after consultation of the *Conseil supérieur de la magistrature* (Judicial Service Commission).

I wish to finish by saying a few words about the status and the structures of the *Ecole nationale de la magistrature*.

The ENM is a public institution attached to the Ministry of Justice.

It has a Governing Board chaired by the First President of the Court of Cassation and the Vice-Chair is the Principal State Prosecutor. It also includes a member of the *Conseil d'Etat*, a lawyer, two professors of law, a well known non-legal personality, three judges and four elected legal trainees.

There is also an education committee.

The institution has its own budget funded mainly by an annual subsidy from the Ministry of Justice.

FRF 150 million in 1993 (80% accounted for by the wage bill).

The 8 members of the administration and the 21 lecturers are judges released from their normal duties.

The permanent teaching staff are all experienced judges seconded to the ENM for an average of three to five years.

However the ENM also calls upon the services of many outside lecturers and teachers for the initial training.

In 1994, for example, 155 external teachers took part in the first stage of training; three-quarters of these were not judges.

The director is appointed by the President of the Republic and is assisted by:

- a director of initial training;
- a director of in-service training;
- three assistant directors;
- a secretary general.

The ENM also employs 83 civil servants.

The ENM has two schools, one in Bordeaux (administration and initial training), and one in Paris, which includes the Division of In-Service Training.

The French experience can be summarised as follows:

After a very modest beginning — only a few dozen judges were given initial training every year (from 1958 to 1979) — the school introduced a parallel course of in-service training for practising judges in 1970.

The approach adopted has, however, always been empirical and progressive, for just as there is no ideal model of a judge, there is no ideal school.

BASIC TRAINING : CONTENT AND METHODS, DURATION OF THE VARIOUS PHASES

Report presented by
Joep J.I. VERBURG
Principal of the Stichting Studiecentrum Rechtspleging

Following selection, future members of the judiciary must follow a training programme. The training programme for the young trainees has a long history; it provides a balance of theory and practice and a structure that has proved worthwhile. For the young trainees a six year programme has been developed; the training programme for outside jurists is much shorter and specifically tailored to their previous experience.

It is thought necessary that the training of judges and public prosecutors is of an independent nature. The conclusion of this is that our trainees, especially the young jurists training to be judge or public prosecutor, must be trained not only in matters of law but are also encouraged to balance the rule of law, their own ideas, those of their colleagues and society.

Without a doubt this training, not only in the field of law but also in the development of the above areas, is one of the main tasks of the Stichting Studiecentrum Rechtspleging (SSR) - the study centre for the judiciary in the Netherlands.

SSR is an independent foundation: emphasising the independence of the judiciary, its schooling and training. It has its own budget, more or less adequately provided by the Minister of Justice.

Through the SSR the judiciary itself arranges the training of future judges and future public prosecutors as well as arranging the ongoing education of judges and public prosecutors.

SSR has a board of members consisting of a chairman, a member of the Supreme Court or the public prosecutors' department at the Supreme Court, three experienced and high-ranking members of the judiciary, a trainee, a senior representative of the Ministry of Justice, a director of one of the 19 judicial services departments and finally a representative from the "outside world", (at this moment a member of the Rotterdam bar). The board is a policy-making and supervising body.

The daily business is dealt with by the so-called "principal", (at present myself) who is a member of the sitting judiciary released from regular duties for 5 years. Under my responsibility a professional course director from outside the judiciary is managing the course programme. To carry out this task he has a number of course managers, partly recruited from the judiciary for a limited period (2/3 years, halftime).

Their task is to compose and implement a sound, well-considered and well-balanced course programme. With regard to its organisation and functioning the SSR is an organ of the judiciary and not of the Ministry of Justice.

The SSR does not have its own teaching staff. Course teachers are recruited from the judiciary, the Bar, the law faculties of the Dutch universities, the State Council, police departments, several ministries as well as from private management consultants. They all have one thing in common - they are excellent teachers. The premises of the institute are based in a small town in the eastern part of the Netherlands, 180 kilometres from the Ministry of Justice. The physical distance underlines its independence.

The training of young trainees normally takes 6 years - the first 4 years at one of the 19 district courts and its public prosecutors' office, with the last 2 years outside the court system outside the judiciary (e.g at the Bar, as a company lawyer, in the police organisation or as a temporary employee in the Secretariat of the European Commission for Human Rights or in the Cabinet of a Dutch member of the Luxembourg Court). This on-the-job training programme is supported by a theoretical course programme, which takes place in the training institute in Zutphen.

Every trainee is obliged to follow a certain number of courses some of which they can choose for themselves. Others are specially developed for them and are therefore exclusive and obligatory.

Technical courses such as the technique of writing judgments, sentences and writing indictments; courses on the organisation of the judiciary, including management principles. Courses about communication techniques and hearing witnesses are obligatory.

The trainee should collect at least 6 course points a year. The courses have a grading system ranging from half a point to a maximum of 2 points depending on the length and the nature of the course.

SSR has developed a standard training programme for the first 4 years which is accepted by the courts and the public prosecutors' office.

The programme during the first 3 years is as follows:

- 6 months as a clerk in criminal chambers of the court,
- 10 months as a clerk in civil chambers of the court,
- 10 months as a clerk in administrative chambers of the court,
- 10 months as a public prosecutor in training.

At the start of each of these training periods there is an obligatory course on the subject and the techniques applicable to that sector of the court or the public prosecutors' office.

At the court the trainee works as a clerk. In fact he is more than that. In addition to the drafting of judgments he also learns to examine witnesses in the presence of an experienced judge. This means that although the trainee has no judicial authority during this period, he should perform much of the judge's work under the care and supervision of a judge. In the public prosecutors' office the trainee works as a deputy public prosecutor and is vested with the regular legal authority. The trainee begins by working with minor offences (e.g negotiating with the police etc) and by the end of the training the trainee more or less independently manages criminal cases. In those three years the trainee receives 3 formal assessments in relation to his work. If the results are poor the trainee has a second chance. If the next assessment is still poor the training stops.

There are some 250 trainees. Each year, one or two trainees leave the training programme compulsorily, and a further one or two trainees leave voluntarily.

After the third year the trainee has to choose whether to become a judge or a public prosecutor. The fourth year of the training is adjusted accordingly. The trainee who is aiming for the sitting judiciary is appointed as deputy judge. The trainee who prefers a career in the public prosecutor's office continues his training as a deputy. The trainee can make suggestions on how he/she wishes to pursue the last 2 years of training outside the judiciary. The criteria for the external traineeship are: law related activities, a certain independence in carrying out those activities in an adequate position in the organisation and a clear description of the function. The principal of the SSR is consulted by the Minister of Justice if this proposal is acceptable or not. We can adopt a critical stance since during this period the salary of the trainee is fully paid by the government.

When the principal of the SSR agrees with the proposal, the Minister of Justice always accepts it. During the training the principal of the SSR looks after the proper execution of the training programme. To evaluate the implementation of the programme the principal visits the courts and the public prosecutors' office every year.

He has talks with the trainees, the court president, the chief public prosecutor, the tutors and the mentor. Each trainee has a mentor to look after him and to watch the on-the-job training. Twice a year a meeting of all mentors and tutors takes place in the training centre in Zutphen.

The training is guided from a central point. This gives all the trainees the same chances, and guarantees that the trainee from the Rotterdam district for example, has been trained to the same standards as a trainee from the Amsterdam district or a small provincial district. As a result of this uniformity and within a certain range, every trainee who has successfully concluded the programme has the chance to be appointed to any district.

In relation to the length of the training programme the trainee who is admitted at an older age - but still below the age of 30 years - has by this stage normally gained some work experience. This may be in the legal field or elsewhere. The principal may reduce the training period but only that 2 year period outside the judiciary and, as an exception, that of the fourth year. The first 3 years would not be altered.

The board of SSR has recently established a committee for the evaluation of the initial training. Special attention will be given to the duration of the various parts of the training and the necessity of the outside training period.

The basic training of the outside jurists is more difficult and is currently less well organised than the training of the young trainees. There is little difference in the experience of the young trainess, but not so with the outside jurists. This is one of the reasons why it is rather difficult to propose a uniform training system. Following selection, when the committee considers a candidate suitable for the judiciary, the candidate will receive training at a court or public prosecutors' office. To access the court of his preference the trainee has to pass another internal examination of that court. For some time the courts were independent in the training they gave and this resulted in 19 different forms of training.

There was much uncertainty in relation to outside jurists and according to research reports 50% of them failed during the on-the-job training, despite the fact that the selection committee considered them suitable to work as a judge or public prosecutor. As a rule the courts ask for the appointment of the candidate as deputy judge. Although it was not certain that the court would accept trainees following training as a judge, most did not give up their job but worked, for instance, 1 day a week for the court.

There was no uniform system of judging performance. Sometimes it would take years for the candidate to be informed that the court would not recommend them to the Minister of Justice to become a judge. To end this uncertainty in training and its unpleasant consequences, a standard framework is to be set up on the basis of SSR proposals which have been approved by the Minister of Justice and the Dutch association for the judiciary. We hope that the proposed system will be adopted and implemented next year. This programme gives a uniform system of training, with the possibility of alterations according to the candidate's experience. It contains on-the-job training and theoretical courses. The most important element of this training is the period after one year of training, which includes several courses about judgments, techniques etc. Here, the district court must decide whether or not the candidate will be recommended. Following this, the training can continue. Formal appointment often takes more than 6 months.

Recently there have been fewer difficulties with the on-the-job training of outside jurists becoming public prosecutor. This on-the-job training is only possible in a full time setting. During one year the outside jurist works as a deputy public prosecutor. His on the job training programme is very similar to the programme followed by the young trainees during their 10 months at the public prosecutors' office. After this year the outside jurist will be appointed as public prosecutor.

THE TRAINING OF JUDGES AND PUBLIC PROSECUTORS

Report presented by
José António MESQUITA
Director of Studies at the Centre for Judicial Studies

1. The training of judges and public prosecutors is carried out by the *Centro de Estudos Judiciários* (the Centre for Judicial Studies), an institution endowed with judicial status and financially and administratively independent, set up as a department of the Ministry of Justice under the Decree Law Nº. 374-A/79 of 10 September.

For many years the traditional system for judges was based on the initial stages of the career structure of public prosecutor, whereby entrance was gained by means of a competitive selection procedure following a training period of six months, and progressed through a series of levels (3rd, 2nd and 1st). Entrance to the career of judge was also gained through a competitive selection procedure (with written and oral tests and a written paper) and progressed also through different levels to promotion to the *Tribunal da Relação* (Court of Appeal) as an appeal court judge and finally to the *Supremo Tribunal de Justiça* (Supreme Court of Justice) as a supreme court judge.

Positions within the hierarchy of public prosecutor were filled, on commission of service, by judges.

Thus, the career of public prosecutor, which lasted on average six years, was in fact a preliminary stage to the career of judge. No one could remain indefinitely in the category of public prosecutor as those who did not take part in the selection procedure for the position of judge on two consecutive occasions, (the selection procedures were opened annually) and those who failed to be appointed on two consecutive occasions, would be eliminated from this career.

Once the autonomy of the career of judges and public prosecutors had been established, allowing them to be separate and independent from each other and yet parallel, a basic change in the training of the respective careers was needed.

A first attempt instituted by Decree- Law no. 714/75 of December 20 introduced the system of training in court ,accompanied by some theoretical sessions. This proved to be deficient and was abandoned after a brief period and replaced by the present system of professional institutionalised training, initiated in 1980, and which has been maintained without any substantial alterations up to the present day.

2. The new system, introduced through the founding of the *Centro de Estudos Judiciários* (Centre for Judicial Studies), was inspired by the French model at the National School of Magistrature and has continued to evolve in a creative and dynamic

form due to the continuous improvement and evaluation of a theory of training for judges and public prosecutors.

The aim, content and methodology, as elements of this theory, were established from the very beginning and, although having essentially remained the same, they have been enriched and renewed by a process of comprehensive and thoughtful evaluation.

In accordance with this idea the *Centro de Estudos Judiciários* has placed its objectives within a series of actions which, in a global and integrated form, aim to structure, invigorate and develop the whole system of the administration of justice in a line of progress and adaptation to the requirements of our present time, which is marked by deep and constant mutations, with obvious repercussions within the system.

3. Set up as a department of the Ministry of Justice for practical and functional reasons, the actual functioning of the centre is deeply rooted in the idea of active participation of judges and public prosecutors, whether individually or through their High Councils. Thus :

- The *Conselho de Gestão* (The Management Board -the organ which defines the main lines of performance in that it is responsible for , among other things, approving the Internal Regulations and the Annual Programme of Activities, appraising the plan for the Budget and the Report of Activities and considering the nomination of members to the executive body) is presided over by the President of the Supreme Court of Justice, who is simultaneously and by nature of his or her functions President of the High Council of the Bench. It includes the Attorney General of the Republic, a judge and a public prosecutor nominated by their respective High Councils, four individuals of recognised merit nominated by Parliament, two professors from the Law Faculty and two *auditores de justiça* (trainees from the Centre) elected by their peers, leaving only the Director of the Centre and the General Director of Judicial Services as members appointed by the Minister of Justice.

- In the same way the *Conselho Pedagógico* (Pedagogic Board) and the *Conselho de Disciplina* (Disciplinary Board) are made up of representatives from the High Council of the Bench and from the High Council of Public Prosecution.

The directors and teaching staff are recruited from amongst judges or public prosecutors.

Finally the training placements in court are tutored by judges and public prosecutors.

4. To be admitted to the Centre candidates must successfully pass an admission test composed of written and oral tests of a technical and cultural nature. Doctors in Law are exempted from the tests and lawyers, registrars, public notaries and judicial officers are required to take only two oral tests. Successful candidates attend the Centre as *auditores de justiça* (trainees) and benefit from, among other privileges, a grant

corresponding to 50% of a judge or public prosecutor's earnings at the beginning of his or her career. Professional training, once initiated, is comprised of activities related to:

- initial training;

- complementary training, obligatory during the first five years;

- permanent training, throughout the whole career, but which is optional.

Initial training is composed of the following successive stages:

- a period of theoretical and practical activities at the Centre, lasting 10 months (15/9 to 15/7);

- an initial trainee placement in court lasting 10 months;

- a second placement in court as a judge or public prosecutor in training lasting 8 1\2 months (15/9 to 31/59).

5. The theoretical and practical phase takes place at the centre in Lisbon, although at this stage contacts and visits of some duration are made to courts, police headquarters, prisons, institutions for minors, notary and registry offices, lawyers practices, companies etc. in various parts of the country.

It is however at the headquarters in Lisbon where training activities for the theoretical and practical phase really take place.

This phase embodies both the technical and the practical in that it aims to provide integrated and professional training developing technical theory from practical questions and dealing with concrete cases that have passed through the judicial process. Simulations of various judicial activities are carried out, namely mock trials in which judges and public prosecutors in training act out the roles of judge, public prosecutor, lawyers, defendants, plaintiffs, witnesses, experts etc. These simulations are recorded on video and later examined during sessions.

This theoretical and practical stage is common to both judges and public prosecutors. It is only after completion of the initial training stage that the option is made to pursue one of these careers.

6. The subjects taken in this theoretical and practical phase are distributed into four jurisdictions: civil jurisdiction, penal jurisdiction, labour jurisdiction, and minors and family jurisdiction.

The sessions are administered by judges or public prosecutors, appointed full or part time as teachers at the Centre for Judicial Studies. The trainees are distributed into groups with a maximum of twelve members.

7.   Simultaneously and in co-ordination with these four legal jurisdictions there are weekly sessions on judicial law aimed at the comprehensive study of the application of the law. Establishing a permanent relationship between the law and social reality opens the way to other perspectives besides the juridical, and assures a critical understanding of the law and an analysis of the statute and role of judges and public prosecutors in modern society, as well as their deontological relationship with the citizen and the other members of the judiciary. In order to encourage the active and critical involvement of the trainees, subjects from as wide an area as possible are dealt with, including judicial sociology and psychology, criminology, ethics and deontology, methodology of law enforcement, the use of experts in court, skills of argument, grounds for judicial decisions, enforcement of penalties, interpersonal relationships etc.

These subjects are presented by experts from different areas, usually coming from outside the Centre for Judicial Studies, and who are often university professors.

8.   In addition there are also weekly sessions, sessions at the end of the day, short courses, seminars, conferences, and study cycles on different subjects including constitutional law, administrative law, community law, Human rights, forensic medicine, data processing, along with subjects of a cultural nature, from the cinema and theatre to other areas of arts and literature.

9.   Once the theoretical and practical phase has been completed, during which the trainees will have undergone a continuous evaluation, the Pedagogic Board classifies and grades them, determining whether they will pass on to the next phase or not.

At this stage successful trainees will declare their option for the career of judge or public prosecutor, compliance of this option being dependant on the number of places available (previously determined by the High Councils) and the grades obtained in the theoretical practical phase.

10.   The following phase, an initial trainee placement in court, begins on 15 September and lasts until 15 July, already taking place in judicial courts under the supervision of a judge or public prosecutor, according to which career the trainee wishes to pursue. During this phase trainees on placement take part in judicial activities under the supervision of a judge or public prosecutor. They can assist in acts of investigation or criminal instruction, help to draw up judicial orders and other decisions, be present during the deliberations of the judicial organs and take part in the preparatory acts of the cases.

At the end of this initial placement an assessment report by the supervising judge or public prosecutor is presented to the directors of the placement, who present this report to the Pedagogic Board. The Board makes a further evaluation, classifying and grading the trainee or deciding on his or her elimination.

As we can see, trainees are subjected to a process of continuous evaluation also during the initial placement which can, as in the theoretical and practical phase, be eliminatory depending on the decision of the Pedagogic Board.

11.   Successful trainees are then appointed as judges or public prosecutors in training by the High Council of the Bench or by the High Council of Public Prosecution.This phase (*éstagio de pré-afectação*) begins on 15 September and lasts until 31 May. During this final placement candidates are responsible (with the assistance of judges and public prosecutors) for carrying out the functions inherent to their respective careers, holding rights and privileges (including earnings), and being subject to the same duties and professional restrictions as a judge or public prosecutor.

In this case, it is the respective High Councils of the Bench and Public Prosecution who assess the merit of each candidate, and who, in case of any doubts as to the ability of the candidate, can order extra inspections.

Having completed the final placement, successful candidates are appointed to full status of judge or public prosecutor, taking part in a mandatory complementary training course which lasts for five years. This is followed by in-service training, which is optional and takes place every year on various subjects - this will be a topic of further discussion.

IN-SERVICE TRAINING: CONTENT, METHODS AND EVALUATION OF RESULTS

Report presented by
Helmut PALDER
Senior Official in the Bavarian State Ministry of Justice

Germany is a federal state. Apart from the juridiction of the Federal Supreme Courts, juridiction lies with the *Länder*.

The judicial system includes the courts and the public prosecutors'offices. Hence, the majority of judges and public prosecutors are in the employ of the *Länder*. Consequently, advanced training for judges and public prosecutors is carried out within a federal structure. This means that each *Land* conducts its own advanced-training programmes for its judges and public prosecutors. Smaller *Länder* will at times co-operate with other states of the Federal Republic.

There is no central advanced-training institution offered by the Federal Republic to all judges and public prosecutors in Germany. There is, however, the German Academy of the Judiciary. Its existence is based on an administrative agreement between the Federal Republic and the *Länder*, dating from January 1 1973. Therefore, the advanced training of judges and public prosecutors in Germany is divided into two areas:

- advanced training conducted individually by each *Land*;

- advanced training offered by the German Academy of the Judiciary.

1. The German Academy of the Judiciary - Advanced Training

This was established on January 1 1973, by virtue of an administrative agreement concluded between the Ministers of Justice of both the Federal Republic and the *Länder*.

At that time, a conference centre was established at Trier. The aim was to focus advanced-training activities of the individual *Länder*, thus, rendering advanced training more effective and creating a venue for judges and public prosecutors in Germany enabling them to meet and discuss professional issues and exchange knowledge.

Following the reunification of Germany, the new *Länder* were included in the administrative agreement in 1993. Wustrau near Berlin was added as a second conference centre. The German Academy of the Judiciary now has two conference centres organising advanced-training programmes for judges and public prosecutors from all courts throughout Germany.

Funding of the German Academy of the Judiciary is divided equally between the federal budget and the *Länder* budgets. The share of the funding package borne by each *Land* corresponds to its size and is determined in accordance with a particular formula. No conference fees are raised. Regular attendees enjoy free board and lodging. Their travelling expenses are (with a few exceptions) refunded by the judicial administrations that delegated them.

The Academy is managed by a director; it has its own personnel dealing with the organisational aspects of the conferences.

It is not incumbent on the Academy to determine the contents of conferences; this is the sole responsibility of the Federal Republic and of the *Länder* organising the conferences. The number of conferences staged by the *Länder* is also dependant on the funding formula mentioned earlier. The number of participants apportioned to each *Land* will also be determined in accordance with this formula.

a) Number and Duration of Conferences

In 1995, a total of 113 conferences will be organised.

In addition, there will be 16 conferences designed particularly for judges and public prosecutors from the new *Länder*. These will be staged for a limited number of years.

For 1994, the figures were approximately the same. A total of 4,165 judges and public prosecutors attended, the average number of participants thus being 36.8. The capacity utilisation rate is 86.2%.

Sessions last between 3 and 9 days excluding the days for arrival and departure. As journeys are often long there is no point in staging even shorter conferences. When longer conferences were advertised in the past it became increasingly difficult to attract a sufficient response.

Many judges and public prosecutors feel that they should not be off work for two weeks just to attend a conference.

b) The subjects for these conferences will be determined by mutual agreement at the programme meetings convened twice annually. At such meetings, the Federal Republic of Germany and all *Länder* are entitled to one vote each, regardless of their size.

Three non-voting representatives of professional organisations act in an advisory capacity. The chairmanship in these programme meetings rotates annually.

During a programme meeting, the Federal Republic and the *Länder* will make proposals as to the conferences they wish to organise next year. Following this, a resolution will be passed on these proposals.

The topics for 1996 were to a large extent determined as early as March of this year. Individual organisational matters and the exact timing will be decided in June of this year. For 1996, topics of civil and criminal law will each comprise approximately 20% of the agenda; for expert juridictions (i.e., administrative courts, labour courts, social courts, fiscal courts), another 20% has been reserved; interdisciplinary conferences on social competence will comprise 15% of the agenda.

What individual topics are behind these figures?

aa) Expert topics from the realm of the classical judicial system comprise approximately 40% of the conference subjects.

In civil law topics examples include "Private Construction Law", "Topical Issues Pertaining to Landlord and Tenant Law" and "Banking Law".

In criminal law topics examples include "Trends and Developments in Criminal Law", "Investigation Techniques and Tactics", "Environmental Criminal Law" and "Organised Crime".

bb) Topics for specialist courts could be "Political-Asylum Law", a topic addressed to administrative judges; or "Law on Registered Physicians and Health-Insurance Law", a topic that may be of interest to judges on social courts.

cc) Interdisciplinary conferences occupy an important place on the agenda.

They deal with such interdisciplinary topics as "Medicine and Law" or "Literature and Law", "Images of the Judiciary in Germany and Its European Neighbour Countries", or "the Judicial System and the Media".

These topics are not attributed to any particular field but are offered to interested judges and public prosecutors from all courts. In addition, the German Academy of the Judiciary does not only intend to impart expert knowledge, but also aims to offer topics for further consideration (which may expand one's immediate professional horizon).

This follows its claim to be an academy. Its encounters with representatives from other professions, particularly physicians, men of letters, and psychologists are valued highly and are perceived to be enriching by German judges and public prosecutors.

dd) The last group (i.e., the conferences designed to impart "social" competence) are held only occasionally. In recent years however they have become more frequent.

These conferences manage such topics as communication in everyday professional life and the organisation of criminal or civil proceedings. They may also provide assistance for handling everyday professional life more efficiently, or address questions of personnel management. In this context, we believe that the future of advanced training within the judicial system still has many tasks to perform.

For Bavaria and the other *Länder* in Germany, while we are satisfied with the professional competence of our judges and public prosecutors, we still have to do more for their social competence.

For many years private companies have recognised the potential in human resources. They perceive appropriate advanced-training conferences as something self-evident, for both self-management and personnel management.

We believe that in some areas of the judicial system the problems are not the same but are similar.

ee) There are no statistics with regard to conferences on European law nor to conferences with an international frame of reference.

It is in the area of European law, or the law of the European Communities that the 1995 programme of the German Academy of the Judiciary offers three conferences.

This may seem a small number but it should be taken into account that topics of European law are regularly found on the agenda of specialist conferences. Thus for instance, it is a matter of course that a conference on "New Developments in Civil Law" will also address the impact of European law on national civil law.

Eight conferences with an international dimension (such as International Family Law, Joint German-French Conference, Comparative Law in civil Proceedings) can be counted for 1995. This type of conference is also on the increase.

c) The type of a conference will often govern the way in which it is conducted.

Conferences that are designed exclusively to impart professional knowledge are frequently held in traditional form (i.e with a lecture followed by discussion). There are also an increasing number of different approaches being taken, be it a panel discussion, group work by the participants themselves, presentation, use of video technology, etc.

The conference centres of the German Academy of the Judiciary meet all the spatial and technical requirements for ensuring that a variety of methods can be adopted.

This aspect has recently become increasingly important. Conferences will be evaluated by participants using a questionnaire. These questionnaires ask for feedback on the contents as well as the methods used by each person presenting a paper.

In this context most of the criticism does not refer to the content but to the method of presentation. For the ministries of justice organising the conferences, evaluation by participants represents a valuable support in deciding whether the respective subject, or the respective person who presented the paper, should be chosen again or not.

In this way, a certain process of self-purification is generated.

d) Of those persons presenting papers, some 60% percent are judges, public prosecutors, or state officials, who are usually higher-ranking; approximately 20% are university teachers, 5% are attorneys and notaries, 10% are from other legal professions, and a further 5% are from non-legal professions.

2. Advanced Training Run by the *Länder*

In view of the comprehensive programme offered by the German Academy of the Judiciary, it may be asked whether there is any demand at all for advanced training run by the *Länder*.

This is a question that we should address because some conferences held at the German Academy of the Judiciary have not been filled to capacity.

Surveys conducted among judges and public prosecutors have shown that 75% of those questioned are satisfied with the advanced-training programme offered; the same percentage, however state that they cannot schedule the advanced-training because of their heavy workload. Moreover, judges cannot be compelled to take advanced-training courses. Apart from this, compulsory attendance of an advanced-training course would hardly have any reasonably significant effect.

The significance of state-run advanced-training should not be underestimated. At the beginning of this report, I mentioned the federal structure of Germany. This is the reason why none of the *Länder* would relinquish its right to influence the advanced-training of its judges and public prosecutors.

Therefore, the *Länder* offer an average of 20 advanced-training courses per year (as advanced-training measures on their own).

a) In this context, there are introductory advanced-training for young judges or public prosecutors.

In the individual *Länder*, systems vary in their detail. Introductory conferences, however, are offered in all of them.

Some *Länder* offer them to all judges jointly, regardless of whether they handle civil or criminal cases. Some make a distinction between civil judges, and, public prosecutors and judges in criminal courts (who will jointly receive advanced-training).

Other *Länder* differentiate between civil judges, judges in criminal courts, and public prosecutors. In most instances, young judges regardless of whether they handle civil or criminal cases will have to attend a one-week advanced-training event, approximately three months after entering the service. Here, some indication will be given as to the planning and implementing of hearings in civil cases, or of a trial in a criminal case; moreover, reports will be given concerning the drafting of judgements, settlement in civil proceedings, the activities of examining magistrates and the independence of the judiciary.

Following a further period of six months these young judges will participate in the second part of the introductory conference lasting just under one week. At this event, special problems of taking evidence (particularly of evidence given by witnesses and experts) will be discussed and simulations using video recorders will be conducted under the direction of experienced judges.

In a similar way, young public prosecutors have to attend one-week introductory conferences.

These deal with issues of co-operation with the police, matters of confinement, special problems of preliminary investigation by the public prosecutor, conduct during trial, and the handling of legal remedies.

In the second part of the introductory conference, simulations are staged with emphasis placed being on rhetoric and on the final speech for the prosecution. In Bavaria, rotation in the offices of judge and public prosecutor provides practice for professional beginners during their first years of office. Young judges and public prosecutors will complete a total of four weeks for such introductory courses.

b) Advanced-training conferences offered by the *Länder*, primarily discuss subject-specific topics such as introductory conferences designed for newly-appointed family judges, judges of guardianship courts and public prosecutors specialising in environmental cases.

c) By way of supplement, several *Länder* (including Bavaria) offer conferences designed to enhance social competence, which are intended to meet requirements in the respective *Land*.

In this context, advanced-training is increasingly being related to the court roles of the respective judge or public prosecutor. This does not apply exclusively to the professional field but especially to the area of judicial administration.

For this reason, we have proceeded to selectively address those judges and public prosecutors who might qualify for executive duties, and to assign them with appropriately advanced training.

At a conference for junior executives problems of judicial administration and problems with personnel management are to be addressed. For those who already hold executive positions executive seminars using the services of a private management training contractor are to be conducted.

3. Miscellaneous

a) Regional advanced-training also exists on a smaller scale.

They consist of one-day advanced-training courses dealing with specific topics organised by the respective regional courts or higher regional courts as part of their own responsibility. These courses are however of no particular significance.

b) More extensive advanced-training measures offered to judges and public prosecutors also exist on a federal level and in the *Länder*. This leaves little room for events staged by other supporting institutions.

In individual cases (e.g events organised by the European Law Academy) judges or public prosecutors will be delegated to such advanced-training conferences. Apart from this, they may, as a rule, attend at their own expense events staged by external sponsoring organisations.

I hope that I have been able to give you, with due brevity, an outline of the advanced-training of judges and public prosecutors in Germany, and I thank you for your attention.

CONTINUED TRAINING OF JUDGES AND MAGISTRATES IN SPAIN

Report presented by
José de la MATA AMAYA
General Council of the Judiciary

I. Main principles of the training of judges and magistrates

The permanent training of judges and magistratres is an essential part of the competence which the General Council of the Judiciary has been constitutionally and legally assigned.

Thus, the General Council is responsible for setting up continued training policy objectives and for directing executive action guided to the realization of the specific public interest which professional training represents: the updating of professional skills and qualified competence which are considered suitable for the satisfaction of the purpose institutionally entrusted to the Justice Administration.

Exercising this competence, the General Council has since 1991 made a great effort to develop continued training for judges and magistrates. The last three years allow us to say that many of the activities have already got a high level of institutionalisation and have become stable activities assumed by a large part of the judiciary, who take part in them on a regular basis.

These programmes are not composed of disparate activities (seminars, economic aims, libraries, publications, collaboration agreements with others institutions, etc.). On the contrary, as a whole, they constitute a logical scheme that tries to answer the following characteristics:

1. **Continued training is conceived or imagined as a right and a duty of the judicial career members.**

The continued training of judges responds to a neccessity inherent in the day-to-day carrying out of their jurisdictional function. For that reason, it has a permanent character that lasts throughout the professional life of the judges.

2. **Judicial continued training is specific and different from other Public Administration careers.**

The characteristics of the judicial status, its independence, the object of their study and the peculiarity of their daily work mean that a specific training combining theory and practice must be designed. We try to improve discussion and debate about the possible solutions to cases instead of trying simply to standardize opinions. At the same time, we intend to provide all judges and magistrates with the different solutions reached in others Courts to the same or similar problems and to make available the decisions of the Supreme Court. In all the different topics, we try to give special attention to practical cases instead of analysing theories.

Judicial continued training needs contact with other professionals who can help them in the solution of cases, (doctors, psychologists, architects, social workers, etc.).

For that reason, judicial continued training must not only be theoretical but also directed to particular cases, taking into account the fusion of interests that come together in the solution of any legal dispute.

3.   The voluntary nature of training

In Spain, nowadays, the professional training of judges and magistrates is voluntary, and participation in training activities has no repercussion in the personal or professional career of people who take part in them.

Nevertheless, the L.O. 14/94, that has reformed the Organic Law of the Judiciary 6/1985, has introduced for the first time the obligation of attending training activities when judges or magistrates change jurisdiction.

4.   Collective and individual training

The General Council of the Judiciary is helping and supporting individual training as much as professional training through group activities, where debate with other professionals is encouraged.

In this way, the General Council is making a great effort in the following two topics:

- It has begun an ambitious plan to install Legal Libraries in most of the Courts and other judicial buildings.

- By means of the publishing and diffusion of the courses' contents (about 40 a year) to all judges and magistrates, the General Council is making a great effort to ensure that each judge and magistrate have been examined in the courses.

In this way, the contents of the course do not benefit only to those people who attend, but all the judiciary. In this way, although some 40 judges regularly attend the courses, the whole judiciary can take advantage of the contents of the courses.

5.   Decentralized training

The General Council has approached decidedly a policy of conventions with autonomous regions, because the General Council's powers cannot be understood separated from the autonomous state structure. Among other things, autonomous regions' Governments have an evident interest in the Administration of Justice. Furthermore, the General Council observes in this way the objective of decentralizing training activities, which permits better management, not only because the costs of the activities are reduced, but as well because in such a way it is possible to adapt the activities to the place where the judges and magistrates perform their function, so that they can take part in the activities without affecting their daily work and have the opportunity of discussing specifically topics which are important in each territory.

In this way, the General Council has signed Conventions on the training of judges and magistrates with more than seven autonomous regions, and is negotiating with another two or three.

II. Kind of actions achieved. Training programmes developed

1. State activities

A. *First State Programme*

The main state programme that is developed by the General Council is what we call the "State Plan".

It is implemented each year through approximately 39 courses. They are attended by about 40 judges and magistrates, 5 members of the Public Prosecutor's Department and 5 judicial secretaries.

The contents of each course are published and the books are distributed to all members of the judiciary. Over the last two years more than 60 books have been distributed and 40 more will be sent throughout 1995.

The topics studied in each course are designed by a working group composed of judges, magistrates, judicial associations and members of the General Council. All of them try to include topics in all fields of law (civil, penal, administrative, labour, etc.). The main objective is to include topics in which theoretical aspects and daily practical problems can be studied and discussed.

B. *Second State Programme*

This new programme has three different purposes:

- it is intended to respond to legislative changes produced every year. To meet that end, Working Seminars are organised with all the professional groups involved in applying the law reform;

- on the other hand, Working Conferences on topical subjects that have not been included in the First State Programme are also organised. For instance, during this year 1995 Conferences about the new Penal Code, the new Jury Law, the new juveniles penal law, etc., will be organised;

- finally, every year conferences are organised for each of the different jurisdictions, in order to discuss practical criteria, to analyze common problems and to try to unify the points of view. In this way, conferences for Minors judges, for Civil Register Judges, for Penitentiary Surveillance Judges, etc., are organised.

C.   *Third State Programme*

In this programme, national activities that have as their purpose the opening up of the judiciary to other legal professionals and other social sectors are included, trying in such a way to improve the discussion between judges and members of these groups, so that the analysis of the different problems from different points of view can be guaranteed, facilitating the exchange of experiences with professionals of different specialities through the organisation of multidisciplinary conferences or meetings.

During the last year, conferences were organized in collaboration with the Ministry of Health, Ministry of Culture, Social Affairs Ministry, Spain's Superior Architects Council, Business Agents General Council, etc.

At the same time, the participation of judges and magistrates in meetings, colloquies, conferences and congresses organised by bodies other than the General Council of the Judiciary have been favoured.

In 1995, work placements in different public organisations have been promoted as well, for the first time, with the purpose of getting to know their structure, organisation and internal functioning. In this way, through direct contact between judges and magistrates and persons in charge of these institutions, the problem of the lack of knowledge of the specific functioning of these institutions will be reduced, and an advantageous interchange of criteria and experiences will be encouraged. At the same time, this temporary immersion period in different institutions will be preceded by the delivery of documentation on the institution to all the judges and magistrates who will take part in the experience.

In such a way, the stages that have been planned during this year are:

- Parliament,
- Scientific Police,
- Ministry of Finance,
- Accounts Court,
- Madrid Stock Exchange.

2. Decentralized Training

2.1. *Provinces and Territorial Plans*

In this field, the main principles established by the General Council of the Judiciary are decentralization, flexibility to be able to give a quick answer to problems and the needs detected in each territory, effective participation and subsidiarity with regard to State Plans.

Some 45 Province Plans and 16 Territorial Plans were set up in 1994 to implement these directives, so that only 5 provinces and 1 autonomous region missed that opportunity.

This year, the General Council has concluded that the model of decentralized training is definitely consolidated, because all the national territory is provided with the decentralized activities that have been demanded by judges and magistrates. The concept of the decentralized training programmes is inspired by the principles of decentralization, design of activities by all the judges and magistrates, practical analysis of law application and participation of all legal professions between the rapporteurs.

Despite this, the accumulated experience during these last three years has led the General Council to introduce an important modification in the decentralized training structure in 1995. During these last three years, training has been dissipated in some of the territories and a saturation of information has arisen, caused by an excessive number of activities. All this gives rise to questions in relation to the human and management structure of decentralized training programmes to guarantee its efficiency and permanence. In this manner, the General Council has created a single management system in every Autonomous Region either in collaboration with the Autonomous Government, as it will be explained afterwards, or without that collaboration, with the principal aim of creating a single and systematized training offer to all judges and magistrates.

2.2. *Conventions signed with Autonomous Regions*

In 1992 the General Council began an important and productive collaboration with Autonomous Regions Governments in this field of action. Since then, the General Council has signed agreements with seven Autonomous Regions, that have involved themselves decidedly in the permanent training of judges and magistrates, collaborating not only with the financing of activities, but also with management of them.

To this end, and with a high degree of implementation every year, in 1995 agreements with Autonomous Regions of Andalucia, Galicia, Pais Vasco, Cataluña, Valencia, Murcia y Madrid have been signed and negotiations have been initiated with Canarias, Castilla La Mancha and Extremadura.

In these Agreements, the system of settling the activities is always the same.

A working group made up of Judicial Associations, judges and magistrates experts in different jurisdictions designated by the General Council, members of the Autonomous Region and members of the General Council is created, and this group has as its purpose the setting up of the activities that will be carried out every year.

3. International Relations

Under the impulse of the General Council International Relations Department, the General Council has signed Agreements with Judiciary Government Organs of several Countries, and has frequent relations, among others, with Judges and Magistrates Training Centres of France and Portugal.

Through these contacts, an interchange of knowledge and practical discussion over the different solutions adopted in different Europeans models to the same legal and social problems is excepted.

4. Community Law Training

The General Council approved in 1993 a basic plan of action, introducing an integral Plan of training in Community Law, to be developed from 1993 - 1995.

That plan was a result of the main criteria and agreements approved that year in the meetings organised on the initiative of the Ministries of Justice of the European Union and tries to set up a stable and continuous system of training in Community Law.

The basic lines approved by the General Council deal with different possibilities. Firstly, we tried to create a basic training programme for two years. Furthermore, each year specialized courses on Community Law are also organized. Finally, Community Law aspects are included in all the State Programme Courses.

At the same time, it is considered necessary to train trainers in Community Law, to create a Service of legal documentation on prejudicial questions and, lastly, to grant financial support every year to participate in training activities organised or promoted by other institutions. This activity was emphasised in a favourable way during the last meeting of persons in charge of judges' and magistrates' training programmes in the countries of the European Union.

The next activities that have been developed to implement these programmes are:

- annual monographic specialized Course in collaboration with the University of Granada and European Community Court of Justice;
- Community Law Courses in many of the Territorial Plans and in execution of the Agreements with the Governments of Autonomous Regions;

- financial assistance to judges and magistrates, to allow their participation in Masters and posgraduate courses in Community Law, organized by Spanish Universities and specialized Institutes;

- preparation and dissemination of publications in Community Law.

5. Installation of libraries and data bases in judicial courts

During 1994 and 1995 the investment effort to get the two next things has continued:

- to make judicial libraries accessible to a higher number of judges and magistrates;

- to guarantee the suitable maintenance and conservation of all judicial libraries installed during the last three years.

To meet that objective, all libraries are modernized with the latest publications that are requested by the judges and magistrates themselves in every territory. Furthermore, after the general conditions of installation, security and control have been assured, the plan of installation of new libraries have gone on.

6. Investigation Aims in Spain and other countries

Conscious of the importance of individual training, apart from the libraries plan, budgetary items have been kept back to cover requests for financial assistance from judges and magistrates to carry out specialized studies.

Obviously, the general conditions for obtaining financial assistance have been established by the General Council, and the only limit is that court activity must not be affected by the absence of the judge. In this way, also in the agreements with Autonomous Regions, a part of its budget is reserved to deal with this kind of petition from judges and magistrates who are sent in the respective Autonomous Region.

7. Collaboration with external conferences

We are referring here to a multiplicity of actions developed at the national level in which the General Council contributes by financing, organising or selecting judges or magistrates as speakers on social or legal topics.

IN-SERVICE TRAINING: CONTENT, METHODS AND EVALUATION OF RESULTS

**Report presented by
Daniel LECRUBIER
Deputy Director of the Ecole nationale de la magistrature
and Director of In-Service Training**

Given the time available to us, I am not going to expand on all of the matters covered in the background material but will concentrate on certain points.

Point one:

The rules governing in-service training

There is a "right to in-service training", which has been recognised by law since 1992, although the legal provisions do not specify how long this right lasts.

In-service training really began in 1975 and has therefore been in existence for 20 years.

From that date the rule was that each judge must receive 15 days' mandatory in-service training per year during the first eight years in office and could subsequently receive an optional one week's training per year.

For the past three years this has been reduced to an optional one week's training for all. This reduction is based on a wager that training has become a matter of habit and that there will not be any relapse.

I wish to stress that if the rule making fifteen days' training mandatory during the first eight years in office had not existed, there would never have been any form of in-service training for French judges.

The first reason for this was a state of mind. Judges, and I imagine that the same applies in your countries, tended to consider that they knew a great deal, if not to say everything, and that in-service training was almost superfluous.

The habit has now taken root and the same judges who underwent eight years' in-service training continue to follow further training sessions.

Above all, if the training had not been mandatory those in charge at the courts would never have agreed to allow judges to attend training sessions in view of the courts' workload.

It was only the fact that training was mandatory that made it possible to overcome their resistance. That problem is now a thing of the past, with some exceptions.

However, I do not want there to be any misunderstanding. The obligation was to follow a training course, but the choice of course was in no way mandatory. Judges remained free to follow a course of their choosing. In France professional advancement and access to specialised functions are not conditional on training. On receiving the curriculum we send to each of them, the judges decide for themselves what training course or courses they want to enrol in for the following year. From a pedagogic standpoint, we consider that judges who attend training sessions must be interested in the subject matter and attend because they want to, rather than having it forced on them. I would even say that training should be a pleasure.

In-service training is also an opportunity to catch one's breath in a taxing profession.

We think that no-one knows judges' requirements - if not to say shortcomings - better than the judges themselves.

Naturally, at the in-service training department we are under an obligation to understand what our colleagues' true needs are and to offer them training courses that tie in with their wishes and desires in a professional context.

Sometimes we get things wrong and almost no-one is interested in a given training course. In that case we go back to square one.

I have one last comment on this subject. I think we can adopt this approach because, before undergoing in-service training, all judges have followed an induction course in the basic skills of their profession, with the result that they already master them when they begin their career.

Point two:

Preparation of annual curricula

The in-service training department is responsible for preparing the in-service training curriculum after consulting various parties: the authorities at the Ministry of Justice, the judges' professional unions and associations, colleagues in the Ministry of Justice's other schools or those who teach on the induction course.

We in fact gather comments and suggestions from our colleagues and various outsiders all year round.

With these as a starting point, we then try to build a curriculum meeting a large number of criteria, so varied are judges' needs in terms of in-service training.

The result is then presented to an educational committee and to the governing board of the Ecole Nationale de la Magistrature, which is a public establishment.

As a public establishment we are independent of the ministry, the Court of Cassation, the Conseil Supérieur de la Magistrature (Judicial Service Commission), the bar association and teachers of law, but all of them are represented on our governing board and are free to give us their often justified comments.

I think this is an advantage. We benefit from their guidance while avoiding dependence.

This frees us from any absolute obligation to pass on the ministry's latest priority, or often the priorities of each ministry department, or the most recent fad in terms of case-law or drafting style. We nevertheless have to keep up with general trends, a fact which may seem self-evident.

The teaching teams must be left considerable discretion in the design of curricula.

This is what enables us to offer a balanced curriculum, often including new ideas viewed from a wider angle.

Point three:

The types of training we offer and the underlying philosophy

We propose an array of subjects ranging from general knowledge (the college must enable judges to understand modern-day issues; we therefore have sessions on Islam and the Arab world and on the problems of bioethics) to more judicial or technical concerns.

Even in the latter case we always attempt to situate technical problems in their general context.

However, knowledge of the law and even understanding of its context do not suffice. A judge is not merely a legal specialist. The profession of judge is a very special one. Judicial practice, compliance with the adversarial principle, methods used in considering judgments, the reasoning behind a decision - in short the very act of passing judgment - call for in-depth training.

A judge is also a communicator and a listener. Psychological and communication skills are essential, and judges must be given assistance in these areas. For this reason we also run courses on oral expression, interview techniques, communication and how to deal with the media.

Judges sometimes also have administrative responsibilities, at least where they are in charge of a court or a department. We try to offer them suitable training sessions covering administrative management techniques, information technology management, team leadership, etc.

In addition to these core training sessions, we design special training sessions taking into account significant changes in the law (but not when an amendment's only purpose is to allow the minister to get his picture in the newspapers).

We also systematically offer judges who change posts, for instance from a juvenile court to an ordinary court, training sessions enabling them to update their knowledge.

All newly appointed court presidents are also given the opportunity of attending a special two week training course.

To sum up, in-service training attempts to keep pace with social and legislative changes and also with the changing profiles of the judges themselves and the judicial institution.

Our fundamental aim is to investigate each subject to the full - and even the most difficult subjects have to be covered -to show all of its facets (history, comparisons and research are useful to us in this respect). We likewise always try to bring to the fore the different sides of a problem and even any conflicting views on it.

Judges then make up their own minds.

The college must not have its own doctrine, but must allow judges to form their own opinions.

Point four:

How training sessions are organised

Training mainly takes the form of one-week courses attended by judges from all over the country. I wish to stress the national nature of these courses since the reasons behind it are important.

Apart from any quality-related issues, it is necessary from a pedagogic point of view that the training venue should allow judges to take a break from their place of work and their day-to-day concerns. Without such a break, training is very difficult. Training must be an opportunity for a breather.

Sessions are held on the college's own premises in Paris. They often involve contributions from a number of speakers on the basis of a programme we have defined, sometimes interspersed with films or case studies, which are worked on in either small classrooms or the lecture theatre.

Practical training is dispensed in firms and institutions such as the National Assembly, the Court of Cassation or the European organisations. Training can also take place on the premises of television or press companies or in hospitals.

Some training sessions are proposed by the college and others are based on the judge's own suggestions, which we accept if they are reasonable.

In recent years we have attempted to vary training arrangements by setting up series of five, six or seven two-day sessions per year on important topics. This makes it possible to give a subject truly in-depth coverage and to work on it between sessions.

In some cases we have established genuine training streams. For instance, on the subject of community law we have courses on two levels, followed by a series of training sessions.

We organise conferences on subjects which are topical within the judiciary or which concern it and arrange "get-togethers" with people from other professional backgrounds, associations, judges of the commercial courts or the Court of Audit and Prefects.

We consider that it comes within the college's role to promote the opening up of the judicial profession to the outside world, not only in terms of thought processes but also through direct contacts.

We increasingly not only open our sessions to a broader spectrum of trainees than judges alone, but also organise training activities jointly with various partners such as the police, educators, the bar associations, etc.

Lastly, we make great efforts to keep in touch with the judiciary elsewhere in Europe.

Point five:

Management and teaching

In 1994 I was one of four judges with responsibility for managing over 900 in-service training sessions, in which over 4,600 judges took part.

As you will have grasped, we are not teaching specialists but organisers.

Each of our training sessions is entrusted to a course leader, who may be a teacher, a judge or frequently a professional such as a journalist or a doctor - in other words someone who is entirely familiar with the subject-matter and who can call on specialists in fields of which we have scant knowledge.

We work with the course leader to define the session's programme, what should be dealt with and how, and together seek out the most suitable speakers. It is the course leader who manages the training session.

The great advantage of such a system is its flexibility and the possibility of adapting it to different situations. We would never have been able to develop in-service training as we have done if we had had our own teaching staff.

Courses live on and sometimes die away. For example, we set up a course on AIDS, which was initially very much in demand, but now after three years enrolment has fallen sharply. It is time to stop but this does not pose any problem.

I might modulate what I have just said. This system does not allow us to gradually amass an in-house expertise. Fortunately, we can rely increasingly on the teaching staff who work on the induction course and on the IHEJ (Institute for Advanced Legal Studies), which is housed on our premises, to obtain in-depth knowledge of a subject, do groundwork, etc.

I might mention the way we manage the financial aspects of our courses. The college wisely decided not to arrange accommodation or meals itself, but to pay a *per diem* to judges, who then fend for themselves. This simplifies matters for us.

Lastly, three years ago we introduced the concept of decentralised in-service training, appointing a judge in each Court of Appeal to act as "training representative". This training takes the form of one-day sessions and is beginning to fulfil its threefold purpose of:

- reaching judges who do not attend the national sessions,

- dealing with subjects of special interest in a regional context, such as forest fires in Corsica and the fishing industry in Brittany, and

- making it possible to work with the judges as a body, rather than as individuals, and with all their local auxiliaries.

Conclusion

In-service training must be a lively, open means of bridging the gap between the judiciary and society, bringing judges a breath of fresh air. It must be a source of inspiration and take into consideration judges' needs while keeping pace with developments in the judiciary and society's expectations of judges as a body.

IN-SERVICE TRAINING: CONTENT, METHODS AND EVALUATION OF THE RESULTS

Report presented by
Joep J.I. VERBURG
Principal of the Stichting Studiecentrum Rechtspleging

The Judiciary and the Parliament (which has to finance it) unanimously agree on the importance of continuing in-service training. This is also organised and carried out by the Stichting Studiecentrum Rechtspleging (SSR).

Target groups for this training are judges, public prosecutors and those people who are training as such (young trainees and outside jurists). There are also some courses in which members of the Bar can participate even though they do not belong to the target group which the SSR has made available. Their participation is expected to enrich or at least brighten training discussions. It must be emphasised that it is only trainees that are obliged to follow some the provided by the SSR. Other members of the judiciary are free to select those courses that they feel appropriate.

Although these courses are not mandatory it is understood throughout the judiciary that it is necessary, both for the general performance of the juridical system and for the development of individual careers to follow relevant courses. For example, an individual's knowledge of management would be taken into account when he applies for promotion to the chairmanship of a chamber or another position for which some managerial skills are useful.

For the members of the judiciary and the trainees, participation in courses is free of charge. The members of the Bar pay a modest contribution.

The SSR programme consists of nearly 150 courses available to members of the judiciary and trainees. They are published annually every April.

The programme for the coming year consists of about 200 courses, 50 of which are exclusively for the juridically trained employees in the offices of the courts and the public prosecutor. The courses which are open to the judiciary are also accessible to judicial trainees. 13 courses are specially developed for the young trainees. Last year over 1400 members of the judiciary entered the programme, 255 young trainees and 550 members of the bar. Of the 5767 course places offered, 5200 were taken up by members of the judiciary.

The SSR has the following policy regarding the composition of the programme.

There are 5 starting points:

1. New developments in statutes or case-law, politics and society. New developments in politics are for example changing ideas in dealing with the drugs problem, abortion, euthanaesia, the environment or with white-collar crime.

New developments in society are in the field of family-life (eg people living together without marrying and the integration of people from different culture). It is often the case that statutes are often too late in adjusting to the changing society.

2. Support for job-rotation among judges and public prosecutors.

The SSR examines which changes are recurring and those which need support. On the basis of this examination the SSR will decide the appropriate training.

Example:

- a public prosecutor is appointed as special prosecutor for cases on the environment cases, of serious fraud, drugs or crimes committed by minors;
- a judge moves to another chamber in the court becoming the instructing judge in criminal matters or bankruptcy;

3. The judicial organisation.

There are courses for newcomers to learn the practical details of the judicial organisation; while it can be assumed they know the relevant statutes, the operational details are not part of university law training.

In addition to this normal training there is, currently, a major reorganisation of the judicial organisation which needs additional explanation. Management skills are therefore given special attention.

4. Refresher courses on legal knowledge.

5. General courses about the philosophy and sociology of law, law and language, legal systems of neighbouring countries and other members of the European Union etc.

To ensure and maintain the quality of this evaluation forms are now being used. These are provided to participants at the end of each course asking their opinion on the content and presentation of their training, and, if they think that their knowledge or ability has improved. In order to offer an interesting programme for the judiciary these forms also invite suggestions for improvement.

The SSR tries to anticipate the long term developments within the judiciary and legislation. For that reason the SSR makes a plan for the years ahead. We obtain useful information from those members of the judiciary who are on secondment at the SSR. On the basis of information and taking into account the specific suggestions of the judiciary itself, the SSR determines for which target group training is necessary and on which subjects. On the basis of this data the SSR draws up the final annual programme.

The courses are not obligatory and there is no way of testing individual results.

Soon, I believe we should develop a mixed system, in which members of the judiciary are obliged to participate in a minimum number of courses followed by a test.

There is no comprehensive explanation for the fact that the Dutch Order of Advocates has started a permanent and obligatory training programme for all members of the Bar and that other staff in the administration of justice are allowed freedom of choice.

In the context of the Themis programme may I inform you finally that SSR also has a specific course in relation to the European Convention of Human Rights which is followed with an annual visit to Strasbourg. Furthermore the SSR offers courses on European Community law plus an annual visit to the European Court.

Recently we have presented a proposal to the European Community to establish a programme for its members to make their judiciaries and public prosecutors more aware of the extent and impact of European law.

FURTHER TRAINING OF JUDGES AND PROSECUTING AUTHORITIES IN PORTUGAL

Report by
Armando LEANDRO
Director of the Centre of Judicial Studies

Each year the *Centro de Estudos Judiciários* organises a further training programme for judges and prosecuting authorities. This training programme is voluntary. However, another type of training exists, the first five years of which are compulsory.

In the interests of decentralisation and to provide a better understanding of the problems of the different regions, further training is carried out both in Lisbon and in different parts of the country.

The goals of training are clearly the enhancement of professional competence, openness to culture and life, reflection on current problems and, while fully respecting the freedom of judges, to promote a further training awareness, ie, to enable judges to adopt a less dogmatic attitude to the complexity of life and need to situate problems within a particular context and to approach them in an inter-institutional, inter-disciplinary and even trans-disciplinary light. The aim then is to create, through the voluntary participation of all concerned, a genuine further training awareness which can continue right up to the end of one's career.

The training programmes are intended for judges and prosecution authorities, although lawyers and other court officials often participate.

With the help of experts from other professions, in particular social workers, probation officers, psychologists, doctors and environment engineers, we are developing projects in the areas of the rights of minors, family law and environmental law. Our intention is to draw on different areas of expertise, different professional cultures and on the interaction between different systems.

A further training programme is drawn up each year and communicated to all judges when the activities of the *Centro de Estudos Judiciarios* begin. Other activities are added to the programme as needs arise. The content of the programme varies. The principle topics dealt with in this year's training programme are: interaction between the judicial system and health in the area of drugs; royalties; banking law; a special course on environmental law which will run throughout the year; commercial companies; bioethics and law; rescuing undertakings and bankruptcy; accidents at work; judicial and non-judicial protection of minors; application by the courts of environmental law in the light of comparative law; international conventions on minors and the family; Community law; electoral litigation.

We naturally follow closely changes in the law which have already taken place or which are under way in order to discuss critically the attitudes which judges and prosecution authorities should adopt in their regard. For example, this year we have already organised various training programmes on the reforms in the areas of civil procedure, the rights of minors and of the family and we shall undertake programmes on the reforms of criminal law and criminal procedure.

We are also attempting to deal with problems of a more cultural nature which affect the operation of the judicial system.

The Centre also publishes studies on judicial topics. This year, at the request of the *Centro de Estudos Judiciários*, the *Centro de Estudos Sociais* of the University of Coimbra completed a study of the administration of justice in Portugal. The results of the study have been published and the study itself has been submitted to judges and lawyers for their comments. The study analyses the actual work of the courts and the way the courts are perceived by the general public. It will be used in various further training programmes as a factual basis for discussion.

We try where possible to publish works on the training programmes. This is an area we are seeking to develop. We recently published several texts on environment law and we shall shortly publish a seminar on commercial companies and on rescuing companies and bankruptcy.

A variety of methods is used in the further training programmes. These include lectures, followed by discussions, seminars and meetings lasting two to three days.

Where possible, we try to adopt an up-to-date, authoritative approach to problems, by inviting academics and other specialists who may or may not be judges. The aim is to open up new dimensions, offer a broader view of problems and to situate them in a cultural and social framework.

We also intend to organise round table discussions on the practical problems which arise or which could arise in the courts. We sometimes invite judges, lawyers and other specialists to lead the debates and to encourage other participants to take part in the discussions.

We are currently trying out several practical further training activities in collaboration with the Supreme Councils. The first of these will be the organisation of a closed seminar outside of Lisbon, in a Lisbon suburb, in collaboration with the Supreme Council of the Prosecution Authorities to discuss problems relating to collecting evidence and criminal investigation. This will be followed by a project with the same goal in the Porto suburbs. We intend to develop further projects of this nature.

We are evaluating further training projects by analysing replies to questionnaires distributed to participants.

Further training is, I am sure, a challenge to which none of us is indifferent. The exchange of information and experiences within the framework of the European network, which we shall undoubtedly set up, could prove very valuable for the future.

CONCLUSIONS

The representatives from the member States of the Council of Europe and candidate States from central and eastern Europe, meeting in Lisbon on 27 and 28 April 1995 to discuss "the training of judges and public prosecutors", held an exchange of views on the conditions of access to the professions of judge and public prosecutor, in the light of a comparative study of the structures and methods existing in the different countries. Furthermore, they examined the methods and content of the different systems of initial and further training of judges and public prosecutors with a view to setting up and developing training programmes in the countries of central and eastern Europe.

In this respect, they reiterated the purpose of the Council of Europe which is to promote and reinforce the principles of a democratic society based on the rule of law and the protection of human rights and emphasised the essential role of the judge as a guardian of individual rights and freedoms guaranteed by the European Convention on Human Rights.

The participants also made reference to the United Nations Basic Principles on the Independence of the Judiciary and to the Recommendation of the Committee of Ministers of the Council of Europe No. R (94) 12 on the independence, efficiency and role of judges and they stressed the link established in both these instruments between the independence of the judicial system and the requirements of the qualities of integrity and competence which guarantee the independence of judges.

They emphasised the reference made in the United Nations Basic Principles on the Independence of the Judiciary to the necessity that "persons selected for judicial office shall be individuals of integrity and ability with appropriate training or qualifications in law" and gave their support to the Recommendation of the Committee of Ministers of the Council of Europe which stresses that the training of judges contributes towards the independence of the judicial power and must provide judges with the theoretical and practical knowledge as well as the professional skills which their functions require.

They indicated their agreement with the principle of this Recommendation according to which any decision concerning the selection and the professional career of judges and public prosecutors should be taken on objective criteria and based on merit, taking into account their qualifications, their integrity and their ability.

They also noted with satisfaction that the Ministers of Justice of the countries of central and eastern Europe who met in Warsaw on 4 April 1995 adopted a Resolution in which they undertake to secure "the conditions for training needed by judges and the legal professions" and to ensure "that these efforts are facilitated by the provision of the necessary human, material and financial resources".

In this respect, they recognised the necessity to give special priority to the training of judges and public prosecutors and expressed the need to extend and improve training methods, taking into account the different legal systems' traditions.

They also recognised that the necessity for judges and public prosecutors to ensure efficiency of justice should not prejudice the requirement of developing the qualifications and the professional conscience of members of the judiciary.

At the end of their exchange of views, the participants expressed the wish to develop and reinforce cooperation at a European level between those persons and bodies responsible for training. Consequently, they agreed to give their support to the creation of a European network for the exchange of information between persons and bodies in charge of the training of judges and public prosecutors.

Those partners who express an interest could, within an informal and flexible framework, exchange information, share experiences and consult with one another to combine their efforts in the area of training. They would thereby have the opportunity of examining together questions relating to training and could, if they so wished, meet to discuss matters of common interest with the aim of finding common solutions.

To facilitate common actions and possible meetings, the Secretariat of the Council of Europe would be happy to act as a point of contact and liaison.

PREPARATORY QUESTIONNAIRE FOR THE MULTILATERAL MEETING ON THE TRAINING OF JUDGES AND PUBLIC PROSECUTORS

(Lisbon, 27-28 April 1995)

I. Requirements for admission to the professions of judge and public prosecutor and initial training

Q.1 Is admission to the professions of judge and public prosecutor in your country on the basis of a competitive entrance exam / recruitment test?

    (a)   judges
    (b)   public prosecutors

If this system does not apply to your country, please go straight to question 8

Q.2 Regarding the competitive entrance exam / recruitment test, please give information on the following points:

1. Body responsible for selecting:

    (a)   judges
    (b)   public prosecutors

2. Requirements for candidates wishing to become:

    (a)   judges
    (b)   public prosecutors

3. Types of tests and skills taken into account in the selection of candidates (please specify if any skills other than legal knowledge are taken into consideration):

    (a)   judges
    (b)   public prosecutors

4. Criteria for evaluating the results of candidates for the position of:

    (a)   judge
    (b)   public prosecutor

Q.3 Do those candidates who have been selected by the competitive entrance exam/ recruitment test gain immediate admission to the profession or do they have to undergo a period of training before admission?

    (a)   judges
    (b)   public prosecutors

Q.4 Where successful candidates gain immediate admission to the profession, please give information on the following points:

1. Does admission entitle the candidate to permanent status or conditional status? In the latter case, who decides whether permanent nomination should be granted or not and what are the criteria for this decision?

    (a)   judges
    (b)   public prosecutors

2. Following admission, will any kind of specific training be given? Please indicate who organises the training, as well as information concerning its duration, content and methodology, in relation to:

    (a)   judges
    (b)   public prosecutors

3. At the beginning of their careers, are there any limits to the functions carried out by:

    (a)   judges?
    (b)   public prosecutors?

Q.5 In cases where selected applicants have to undergo a training period before gaining admission to the professions of judge and public prosecutor, please give information on the following points:

1. Body responsible for training:

    (a)   judges
    (b)   public prosecutors

2. Type of training for:

    (a)   judges
    (b)   public prosecutors

3. Duration of training of:

    (a)   judges
    (b)   public prosecutors

4. Content and methodology of the training of:

    (a)   judges
    (b)   public prosecutors

5. Status of:

    (a)   trainee judges
    (b)   trainee public prosecutors

6. Criteria for evaluating:

    (a)   trainee judges
    (b)   trainee public prosecutors

Q.6 Apart from a formal competitive entrance exam / recruitment test, are there any other ways of gaining admission to the professions of judge and public prosecutor? Please specify, indicating the body responsible for this decision and on what criteria the decision is based.

    (a)   judges
    (b)   public prosecutors

Q.7 Are candidates who gain admission to the professions of judge and public prosecutor other than by means of a formal competitive entrance exam / recruitment test required to undergo specific training?

    (a)   judges
    (b)   public prosecutors

Questions 8 and 9 only apply to those countries in which there is no formal competitive entrance exam / recruitment test

Q.8 If there is no formal competitive entrance exam / recruitment test in your country, please describe the way in which admission to the professions of judge and public prosecutor takes place, indicating the body responsible for this decision and the criteria upon which the decision is based:

    (a)   judges
    (b)   public prosecutors

Q.9 *Is there any kind of training provided in those cases referred to in the previous question? If so, please indicate who organises the training, as well as information concerning its duration, content and methodology, in relation to:*

    (a)   *judges*
    (b)   *public prosecutors*

II.   **Further training of judges and public prosecutors**

Q.10 In your country, is there any permanent training scheme provided for judges and public prosecutors during their career? If so, please indicate:

1. Body responsible for the organisation of the training of:

   (a)   judges
   (b)   public prosecutors

2. Type of activities normally carried out, specifying if these include areas of knowledge other than those that are strictly legal, for:

   (a)   judges
   (b)   public prosecutors

3. Approximate number of training activities organised annually for:

   (a)   judges
   (b)   public prosecutors

4. Is participation in these activities mandatory or voluntary? Please reply in relation to:

   (a)   judges
   (b)   public prosecutors

Q.11   Are there any reforms relating to admission to the profession and/or the training of judges and/or public prosecutors likely to be introduced in the near future? If so, please describe their principal aspects.

Further comments

If necessary, please add any further information concerning the selection, admission and training of judges and public prosecutors in your country which you think may be relevant and should have been included in the questionnaire.

Please enclose along with your answer to the questionnaire the current legislation in your country concerning admission to the profession of judges and public prosecutors and their respective training.

SYNTHESIS OF THE ANSWERS TO THE QUESTIONNAIRE

In order to prepare the multilateral meeting on the training of judges and public prosecutors in Europe, taking place on 27 and 28 April 1995, a questionnaire was sent to the Member States of the Council of Europe and to the non-Member beneficiary States (35 States). The present document, prepared by the Directorate of Legal Affairs, is a synthesis of the answers received from 34 of them.

ALBANIA

I. Requirements for admission to the professions of judge and public prosecutor and initial training

In Albania, judges and public prosecutors are not recruited on the basis of a competitive entrance examination or recruitment test, but are appointed by the High Council of Justice, generally on the basis of a test.

The only requirements that the candidates for these professions must meet are: to have the enjoyment of all of their rights, have a good reputation and have graduated as lawyers.

The High Council of Justice is also responsible for the initial training of judges and public prosecutors.

II. Further training of judges and prosecutors

Further training of judges and prosecutors is only in its early stages in Albania. However, the Justice Ministry is making an effort to improve the qualifications of the persons it employs. For this purpose, a division responsible for training organises regional seminars and periodic tests. Participation in these training activities is mostly voluntary, but it is mandatory in some cases, in particular, those concerning important changes in legislation.

AUSTRIA

I. Requirements for admission to the professions of judge and public prosecutor and initial training

In Austria, persons wishing to be admitted to the office of judge or public prosecutor must take a competitive entrance exam, which is the same for both professions. For this purpose, candidates must apply during the year of training with a court which all persons wanting to enter into a legal profession (including that of lawyer) must complete. After approximately 10 months of training, candidates are invited to take a recruitment test which assesses not only their legal knowledge but also their personality.

Persons wishing to take this recruitment test must fulfil the following requirements: they must have Austrian citizenship, have full legal capacity, fulfill the physical and moral conditions necessary for carrying out the function of judge or public prosecutor, have completed their legal studies in an Austrian University, and have trained at least for nine months in a court. Moreover, as a general rule, they must be under 35, but exceptions may be granted in certain cases.

The recruitment test consists of a written and an oral portion, a psychological test and an interview. The candidates are jointly assessed by the Presidents of the three Courts of Appeal and a panel of judges who rank them according to merit. This ranking list is then transmitted to the Justice Minister who appoints the trainee judges (all persons destined to pursue a career as judges or public prosecutors are appointed as trainee judges; the separation between the two professions takes place at a later stage). Even though it is an unwritten rule, the Minister, in practice, appoints only the candidates who are on the list.

The trainee judges must undergo a three year period of training which is added to the trainee period which they have already completed in one of the courts. This training period includes internships in a professional environment with prosecutors, judges, barristers or notaries and with the Supreme Court or the Justice Ministry. Parallel with this practical training, the trainees are required to take theoretical courses held by experienced judges of the Courts of Appeal or the Supreme Court.

During the training period, the instructors give their written opinions as to the suitability of each trainee judge for the profession of judge/public prosecutor and also give him a final mark. At the end of this period, the trainees must sit a final exam which covers all areas of national law. The successful candidates are then permanently appointed as judges or public prosecutors.

There is also another way to be admitted as a judge/public prosecutor which is reserved for attorneys and public notaries having passed the necessary State exams for the exercise of these professions. It is enough for them to pass an additional examination, for which they need special permission to sit, relating to the subjects specific to the profession of judge/public prosecutor. The requirement of four years of professional legal practice, including one year as a trainee judge, is sine qua non for admission to the profession of judge/public prosecutor.

II. Further training of judges and public prosecutors

Judges and public prosecutors in Austria have many opportunities for further training in the form of courses, seminars, colloquia, and others, organised under the aegis of the Justice Ministry, judges' and public prosecutors' associations, public institutions and private unions.

Every year, the Justice Ministry draws up, in conjunction with the Presidents of the Courts of Appeal and the Attorney General, a training programme comprising approximately 60 colloquia, seminars, courses and conferences relating to strictly legal themes as well as psychological ones. Participation in these training activities is voluntary.

III. Reforms likely to be introduced in the near future

It is probable that no reforms on the subject will be introduced in the near future, as the current system has been established rather recently.

BELARUS

In Belarus, there are no recruitment tests determining access to the professions of judge and public prosecutor.

Some judges, namely the judges of the Supreme Court and those of the Supreme Economic Court, are elected by the Supreme Council (Parliament); the others are appointed by the President of the Republic.

Candidates for the office of judge must be citizens of the Republic of Belarus, be at least 25 years old, must never have committed a dishonourable act, have completed university studies in law, have a minimum of two years of professional experience in the legal field and have passed a qualification exam. It is also possible for persons not meeting the above-mentioned age requirement, but older than 23, to be admitted to the office of judge; however, these judges can only hear administrative disputes and those relating to the execution of judgments.

As for public prosecutors, they are appointed to their posts by the Attorney-General, who is himself elected by the Supreme Council. The only requirements to be met in order to be admitted to this office are to be a citizen of the Republic of Belarus, have no criminal record and have completed university studies in law.

With respect to the initial training of judges and public prosecutors, the legislation of the Republic of Belarus limits itself to stating that persons without adequate experience in the legal field should undergo a training period before taking up their offices. This training period, which for judges is served in courts and for public prosecutors in prosecutors' offices, lasts two years for the former and six months for the latter.

BELGIUM

I. Requirements for admission to the professions of judge and public prosecutor and initial training

In Belgium, admission to the professions of judge and public prosecutor is always based on a recruitment test. This recruitment test is different depending on whether or not the candidates have some professional experience in the legal field. Candidates having no professional experience must take a competitive entrance exam for admission to judicial training, which allows them to be admitted to a three year period of training. Other candidates must fulfil certain requirements and pass a professional aptitude test, after which they may be directly admitted to the profession of judge/public prosecutor.

The body responsible for the selection of candidates for the offices of judge and public prosecutor is the College of Recruitment of Judges/Public Prosecutors, composed of 22 members divided into two juries (one French-speaking, the other Dutch-speaking). Each jury is composed of five members of the judiciary (three judges and two public prosecutors), three university professors and three lawyers.

Persons having either a doctorate or a bachelor's degree in law may take the exam for admission to the judicial training period. Persons taking the professional aptitude exam must possess one of these diplomas and have moreover a certain number of years of experience, varying according to the intended profession:

- candidates for the office of judge (of a court of first instance) must have either ten uninterrupted years of experience at the bar, five years of experience as a Legal Adviser, Junior Officer, Deputy Junior Officer, Auxiliary Judge, Assistant Auxiliary Judge at the *Conseil d'Etat* or at the Arbitration Tribunal, or finally, have been registered for 12 years with the Bar, or have practised for the same period as a public prosecutor, a notary, a legal academic or researcher, or legal functions in a public or private service;

- candidates for the office of deputy public prosecutor must have practised for nine years either as a lawyer, notary, legal academic or researcher or exercised legal functions in a public or private service, or have had five years of experience in the profession of Legal Adviser, Junior Officer, Deputy Junior Officer, Auxiliary Judge, Assistant Auxiliary Judge at the *Conseil d'Etat* or as an Auxiliary Judge at the Arbitration Tribunal.

The competitive entrance exam for the judicial training period consists of a written exam of admissibility to an oral exam determining admission. The written exam consists of drafting a summary and key words, as well as a case comment relating to, at the candidate's choice, one of the following areas: commercial law, civil law, criminal law, constitutional and administrative law, or labour and social security law. It also includes a synthesis and critical analysis of an essay on a subject concerning social, economic, political or cultural aspects of the present-day world in relation with law. Candidates receiving a mark of at least 60% in the whole of the written portion of the exam are admitted. The oral portion of the exam consists of a discussion on all or part of the written portion and a presentation by the candidate on one of the subjects of his choice, excluding the subject chosen for the written portion of the exam. The candidates who receive at least a mark of 60% in both portions of the exam, written and oral, are ranked according to their results. The competitive entrance exam, like the professional aptitude exams, is designed to assess the "maturity" of the candidates and their "intellectual ability to practise the profession" (Art. 259 bis, of the Judicial Code).

The professional aptitude exam also consists of a written and an oral portion. The written exam is made up of an essay on an assigned subject concerning social, economic or cultural aspects of the present-day world in relation with law and the drafting of a judgment in a case whose elements are given to the candidate in the form of a complete file. Here, too, candidates receiving a mark of 60% for the whole of the written exam are declared admissible. The oral exam consists of a critical presentation, made without notes, by the candidate on a subject of his choice in civil or criminal procedure law, oral questions on this presentation and of a discussion on all or part of the written exam. Candidates obtaining a mark of 60% in each of the exams, written and oral, are awarded the certificate of professional aptitude, which enables them to be appointed to the profession of a judge/public prosecutor.

While persons who have been awarded the certificate of professional aptitude may be directly appointed to a post of judge or public prosecutor, those who have passed the competitive entrance exam for trainee judges/public prosecutors must then undergo a three-year period of training, both theoretical and practical: the judicial training period. The body responsible for this training period is an "Advisory Committee", existing in each district of the appeal and labour courts, and composed of the heads of the judges' and the prosecutors' orders of the court of appeal, of the court concerned by the appointment as well as the president of the Bar Association, and, in appropriate cases, of two or three lawyers. This Advisory Committee directs the training period and appoints trainers who are directly responsible for the training of the trainees in each prosecution service belonging to its jurisdiction.

The judicial training period includes theoretical training consisting of a series of lectures organised by the Justice Minister and practical training made up of training periods served in various institutions:

- from the 1st to the 15th month, with a crown prosecutor, and/or with the junior officer of the labour court, and/or the military prosecutor or judge; this period also includes one month with the administrative services of one or more Crown Prosecutor's Office(s);

- from the 16th to the 21st month with a prison, a police service or a notary chamber or an office of bailiffs or with a legal department of a public economic and social institution;

- from the 22nd to the 36th month, with one or more chambers of the court of first instance of labour or commercial matters, or with a military court, this period also including one month with one or more registries.

During the first fifteen months of training, trainees have the status of officers of the criminal police, auxiliaries of the Crown Prosecutor, junior officer in the labour courts or prosecutor at the military court, but they may only exercise their functions under the authorisation of the Attorney General or the Chief Military Prosecutor. After six months of training, they may be authorised by one of these authorities to exercise all or part of the functions of the prosecution service, but only for the duration of the training period. After 15 months of training, the trainee judges may become substitute registrars. Lastly, during the last fifteen months of training which are served with a court or a military court, the trainees assist the judge or judges making up the chamber to which they are assigned and assist in the deliberations without however taking the place of the judges.

II. Further training of judges and public prosecutors

There are no opportunities for further training of judges and public prosecutors in Belgium.

III. Reforms likely to be introduced in the near future

The subject matter has quite recently undergone a reform with the Law of 18 July 1991 amending the rules of the Judicature Code relating to the training and recruitment of judges/public prosecutors. No other amendment is currently on the agenda.

BULGARIA

I. Requirements for admission to the professions of judge and public prosecutor and initial training

Bulgarian judges and public prosecutors are not recruited on the basis of a competitive exam, but are appointed by the Supreme Judicial Council. The candidates must have completed university studies in law and have finished a mandatory training period prescribed by law, have full legal capacity and must not have been convicted to serve time in prison for a crime committed with premeditation. Lastly, they must have the moral and professional standing necessary to exercise the functions of judge/public prosecutor.

The persons who are recruited in the manner described above must undergo a practical training period lasting one year in departmental courts. They are then appointed judges or public prosecutors for a period of two years.

II. Further training of judges and public prosecutors

There are three forms of further training. The first is proposed by the inspection service of the Justice Ministry, which draws up an annual programme. This programme provides for courses lasting several days, relating not only to purely legal themes, but also to ethical ones. Each year, at least two sessions of courses are organised, open to judges and public prosecutors. The participants chosen by the presidents of the courts are required to attend these courses.

Certain training activities are organised on a regional level by the president of each departmental court. In practice, they take the form of meetings between judges of the departmental court and those of regional courts, during which analyses of judicial practice and examination of problems concerning certain gaps in legislation take place.

Finally, the third form of further training involves the participation of judges and public prosecutors in seminars and colloquies organised by other state institutions or by Bulgarian or foreign non-governmental organisations. Participation in these activities is voluntary.

CROATIA

I. Requirements for admission to the professions of judge and public prosecutor and initial training

In Croatia, judges and public prosecutors are not recruited on the basis of results obtained in a competitive entrance exam or in a similar selection test: they are appointed to their post.

It is important to bear in mind that in Croatia, the public prosecution service, although a part of the judicial system, is an autonomous state administration, even if its organisation is modelled on that of the courts.

Judges are appointed for life by the Judicial Service Commission, an independent body whose members are elected for eight years by the Parliament from among experienced jurists. Public prosecutors are appointed for an eight year period, which can be renewed by the Parliament on the request of the Prosecutor General.

Candidates for the post of judge or public prosecutor must fulfil several conditions, some of which are common to both functions: this is true of the conditions relating to croatian nationality and successfully passing an exam which determines aptitude to perform a legal profession, an exam which is the same for judges, public prosecutors, notaries, lawyers, etc. Candidates wishing to become public prosecutors must also possess a certain number of years experience in the legal field, which varies according to the post desired. Candidates wishing to become judges must either have carried out a training period of two years in a court, a public prosecutor's office, a law firm or a notary's office before taking the exam or have practised a legal profession for at least two years after taking the exam.

The exam includes a written test and an oral test and takes place before an examination committee whose members are appointed by the Justice Ministry. The written part of the exam contains tests on criminal law and civil or commercial law. The oral tests are on criminal law, civil law, criminal procedure, civil procedure, commercial law, family law, administrative law, labour law, constitutional law and the organisation of the judiciary.

In order to assist candidates in preparing for this exam, the Justice Ministry and certain lawyers' associations sometimes organise seminars on controversial legal points or, more generally, on exam topics.

II. Further training of judges or public prosecutors

There is no permanent structure in Croatia for the training of judges and public prosecutors. However, various lawyers' associations organise conferences and seminars from time to time, sometimes with the financial support of the Justice Ministry.

III. Reforms likely to be introduced in the near future

At present, there is a draft law on the function of prosecutors which, if adopted, will introduce important changes to the current law of 1977. This draft law provides that only the Prosecutor General will be appointed for eight years, with the possibility of renewal: other public prosecutors will be appointed for an indefinite period. In addition, the body responsible for their appointment will no longer be the Parliament but the Judicial Service Commission, which is already responsible for appointing judges.

CYPRUS

I. Requirements for admission to the professions of judge and public prosecutor and initial training

In Cyprus, judges and public prosecutors are not recruited on the basis of a competitive exam or similar test. The conditions for entering the professions of judge and public prosecutor differ from one another.

Candidates wishing to become judges must have practised law for at least seven years and have an irreproachable reputation. However, lawyers having only five years of professional experience may, as an exception, be appointed to the office of a judge, provided that two-thirds of the members of the second instance court agree. Persons wishing to apply must send a letter declaring their interest accompanied by their *curriculum vitae* to the President of the District Court in which they practise. If the President of this court supports the application, he sends a letter of recommendation to the Judicial Service Commission, which is the body responsible for the appointment of new judges. This Commission is made up of the Attorney-General and judges of the second instance court. Until recently, the Committee appointed the candidates directly to a post of judge, but presently, they are being first called for an interview.

With respect to the public prosecution service, it must be remembered that, in Cyprus, its responsibilities are distributed between two independent authorities: the Attorney-General's office and the police. The persons who, in the Attorney-General's Office, take on the duties of a prosecutor are advocates of the Republic who are admitted to this office after an interview with an Advisory Committee. The Committee is made up of the Attorney- General and senior Advocates of the Republic. The candidates chosen by this Committee must be interviewed again by a Public Service Committee, of which either the Attorney-General or one of his deputies is a member.

In Cyprus, neither initial nor further training is available to judges or public prosecutors.

II. Reforms likely to be introduced in the near future

Only one reform has recently been introduced in Cyprus: that, as mentioned above, of the interview before the appointment of judges.

CZECH REPUBLIC

I. Requirements for admission to the professions of judge and public prosecutor and initial training

In the Czech Republic, there is no recruitment test for admission to the professions of judge and public prosecutor.

Judges and prosecutors are appointed for life: the former by the President of the Republic, and the latter by the Justice Minister upon the proposal of the Attorney General. Applicants for these professions must however meet certain requirements which are the same for both professions: any Czech citizen can be appointed judge or public prosecutor if he is at least 25 years old, enjoys his civil rights, has completed his legal studies and passed a professional examination relating to his legal knowledge and has been judged to be incorruptible and suitable to fill the post for which he applies.

In the majority of cases, persons wishing to become judges or public prosecutors are first appointed as legal trainees by the president of the court to which they are called to exercise their functions. To be appointed as legal trainees, these persons must fulfil the requirements mentioned above, with the exception of those relating to the minimum age and a professional exam. The legal trainees undergo a three year period of training whose goal is to prepare them for the future functions of a judge or public prosecutor.

During this period, the legal trainees undergo training which is organised at two levels: at the national level, it is organised by the Institute for Continuing Education of Judges, which is part of the Justice Ministry. These training activities are open to both trainee judges and trainee public prosecutors; attendance is compulsory. Training is also organised at the regional level by the courts and public prosecutor's offices throughout the country. This training includes seminars, in which judges and prosecutors share their experience, practical cases and simulations.

At the end of this training period, the legal trainees must take the professional exam to assess whether they have acquired the theoretical and practical knowledge necessary for practising the profession of judge/public prosecutor. This exam, organised under the aegis of the Justice Ministry, takes place before a Commission composed of five eminent legal experts. The trainees who have passed this exam are appointed to the post of a judge or public prosecutor.

II. Further training of judges and public prosecutors

Opportunities for further training exist in the Czech Republic for both judges and public prosecutors. It consists of exchanges of views and of experiences, which currently relate primarily to the new legislation. These training activities are organised by the Institute for Continuing Education of Judges: of the approximately forty activities organised annually, approximately 30 are addressed to judges and 10 to public prosecutors. However, there is no strict separation between the activities for judges and for public prosecutors. Attendance is not mandatory, but experience shows that there is a great interest and that demand often exceeds supply.

III. Reforms likely to be introduced in the near future

Reform concerning admission to the professions of judge or public prosecutor and their training is neither in progress nor planned at the moment.

DENMARK

I. Requirements for admission to the professions of judge and public prosecutor and initial training

In Denmark, judges and public prosecutors are not recruited on the basis of a selection exam but are first engaged as deputy judges or assistant police commissioners (the functions of the prosecutors in Denmark are exercised by public prosecutors and police commissioners). After a certain number of years of service, they are appointed to a regular post.

Deputy judges and assistant police commissioners are recruited on the basis of their files and an interview. They then undergo a training period, lasting four years for judges - and served in a district court - and three years for police commissioners. This training consists of a practical and a theoretical part and corresponds to each participant's real level of training.

At the end of this period, the deputy judges are transferred to another district court, and after approximately ten years (in total) of service, they are transferred again, this time to a higher court for a period of nine months.

After the initial three year training period, the trainee public prosecutors undergo another two year training period with an Assistant Public Prosecutor, at the end of which they are transferred again to a police district.

After approximately ten years of service, deputy judges and assistant police commissioners may apply for regular posts. Judges are appointed to such posts by the Queen upon the proposal of the Justice Minister, who acts on the advice of the president of the higher court and the president of the Supreme Court; police commissioners and public prosecutors are appointed by the Justice Minister.

II. Further training of judges and public prosecutors

During their careers, judges and public prosecutors have access to further training which is organised for the former by the Justice Ministry, in collaboration with a deputy judge responsible for training. The Justice Ministry is also responsible for the further training of public prosecutors, but, in practice, it is organised by the Danish Police College.

This further training includes courses and seminars on legal topics as well as computer and management courses (for judges). In 1994, 33 courses were organised for judges. Attendance is voluntary, except for those activities organised in the framework of the initial training, which are compulsory.

III. Reforms likely to be introduced in the near future

Two committees have been set up by the Danish government. One is to examine the recruitment and training of judges; the other, the training of the police and public prosecutors. The former will submit its report at the end of this year; the latter within the next few months. It is therefore possible that reforms based on these reports will be introduced.

ESTONIA

Admission to the professions of judge and prosecutor, as well as their training, are rather distinct in Estonia. These two professions will therefore be treated separately.

A. *The training of judges*

I. Requirements for admission to the profession of judge and initial training

The applicants for the profession of judge must first complete a training period lasting a maximum of two years under the direction of experienced judges or within the Justice Ministry, after which they must pass an exam.

The body responsible for the selection of candidates is the Commission of Examination of Judges, attached to the National Court (the Supreme Court of Estonia) and consisting of three judges of first instance courts, three judges of second instance courts, and three judges of the National Court, a professor of Tartu University and a representative from the Justice Ministry.

The requirements to be met by candidates for the profession of judge - and public prosecutor - are to have Estonian citizenship, to have received higher education at Tartu University or education judged to be equivalent, to be morally irreproachable, and in addition to meet certain age requirements: administrative judges must be at least 24 years old; those of city or district courts, 25 years old; and those of the National Court, at least 30 years old.

The exam relates exclusively to the legal knowledge of the candidates. Successful candidates are presented by the President of the National Court to the President of the Republic who appoints them for an indefinite period to the position of judge in the courts of first and second instance. The National Court Judges are appointed for an indefinite period by Parliament.

Once recruited, new judges must take 2 to 4 days of courses each month organised by the Justice Ministry and the National Court. These courses, held by professors and various legal professionals, cover new laws, court practice and the analysis of the drafting of judgments.

There is another avenue of access to the office of judge: the Commission of Examination of Judges can exempt a person from taking the entrance exam if he has already worked as a judge (under the previous regime), law professor, public prosecutor or in some other position requiring in-depth legal knowledge. In such a case, the person recruited also does not need to undergo any specific training.

II. Further training of judges

In Estonia, there is an annual programme of training for judges which is established by the Justice Ministry, the National Court and the Lawyers' Advanced Training Centre at Tartu University. This programme includes monthly seminars, workshops and courses primarily relating to legal topics. Attendance by judges is voluntary.

III. Reforms likely to be introduced in the near future

Reforms are currently neither in progress nor planned with respect to the admission and training of judges.

B. *The training of public prosecutors*

I. Requirements for admission to the profession of public prosecutor and initial training

The only way to be admitted to the profession of public prosecutor is by an exam organised by the State Prosecutor's Office. The requirements to be met by the candidates are the same as those which apply to candidates for the profession of judge, namely, to have Estonian citizenship, to have higher university education from Tartu University or education judged to be equivalent, and to be morally irreproachable. This exam also relates exclusively to the legal knowledge of the candidates.

The successful candidates are then appointed to the post of public prosecutor by the State Prosecutor who is himself appointed for five years by the Justice Minister. Once appointed, they are not required to undergo any specific training.

II. Further training of public prosecutors

It is the State Prosecutor's Office which is responsible for the further training of the public prosecutors in Estonia. For this purpose, it has empowered the National Court, the Justice Ministry and the Lawyers' Advanced Training Centre at Tartu University to draw up several training programmes consisting of seminars, workshops and courses concerning not only legal topics, but also computers or history. Attendance in these training activities - at least four per year - is mandatory for public prosecutors.

III. Reforms likely to be introduced in the near future

No reforms are currently in progress or envisaged with respect to the recruitment and training of public prosecutors.

FINLAND

I. **Requirements for admission to the professions of judge and public prosecutor and initial training**

In Finland, there is neither a competitive entrance exam nor a recruitment test for entering the professions of judge or public prosecutor.

The judges are appointed by the President of the Republic acting alone (for appointments to the posts of President of the Supreme Court and President of the Supreme Administrative Court) or on the recommendation of various authorities: in practice, the Supreme Court recommends candidates for the posts of judge in this court and for the Presidents of Courts of Appeal; the Supreme Administrative Court recommends the judges to be appointed to its own bench and the County Court judges (the administrative courts of first instance), and each Court of Appeal recommends the candidates for other posts of judge in its own jurisdiction.

With respect to public prosecutors, those attached to police courts are appointed by the Justice Minister; the Police Superintendents - who exercise the role of the prosecution in rural courts - are appointed by the regional governments.

The requirements to be met by candidates vary slightly depending on which office they apply for, but in every case it is required that they hold a university degree in law, have the necessary knowledge for the exercise of their profession and have a certain number of years of experience in judicial functions - this criterion being decisive for filling most of the posts of judges - or professional experience preparing them to exercise judicial functions.

Such experience is acquired through a one year training period with a first instance court. This training period is not mandatory, but recent statistics show that approximately 70% of all practising lawyers in Finland have completed it.

Trainees are appointed by the Court of Appeal competent for the territory concerned on the recommendation of the President of the first instance court wishing to engage them. The content of the training varies from court to court, but as a general rule, the trainees begin by familiarising themselves with the activities of the court, after which they judge non-contentious civil cases and prepare civil and criminal cases before passing them on to the judges. Finally, at the end of their training period, trainees may themselves judge cases. It is usually required that trainees have served as judges for at least ten court sessions. The title of senior lawyer ("*varatuomari*") is conferred by the Court of Appeal upon those who have sucessfully undergone the training period.

II. Further training of judges and public prosecutors

Further training for judges is organised by the Justice Ministry. Further training for public prosecutors is organised jointly by the Justice Ministry and the Public Prosecutor's Department.

The Justice Ministry has recently organised a large scale training scheme for judges concerning the civil procedure reform which entered into force on 1 December 1993. A similar scheme is currently being organised to prepare the judiciary for the future criminal procedure reform. Other training activities are also held relating to European Law, bankruptcy, accounting, communications, foreign languages and management. Last year, 359 days of training were offered to judges.

The courses offered to public prosecutors concerned management, violations of environmental law, accounting and violations relating to labour law. Some public prosecutors have also participated in the training activities relating to the civil and criminal procedure reforms. Last year, thirty days of training were organised for public prosecutors.

The participation of judges and public prosecutors in further training is not strictly mandatory; however, it is expected that they participate in training activities relating to their own field.

III. Reforms likely to be introduced in the near future

A Committee was set up to examine the feasibility of reforming the system of appointment and career prospects of judges. Its main suggestions, which appeared in a report published in October 1994 were the following:

- open the profession of judge to barristers, prosecutors and other lawyers, even if they do not have any experience in judicial functions;

- extend the court training period to two years;

- in the selection and the promotion of judges, replace the criterion of number of years served in the judiciary with criteria relating to the skill and personal merits of the candidates;

- establish a common appointment procedure for all judges and abolish the system of recommendations.

These suggestions have not led to amendments to the legislation in force. It is likely that a new committe will be appointed to further develop the ideas contained in this report.

FRANCE

Preliminary remark:

It should be noted that in France, recruitment and training procedures for administrative judges are completely different from those used for judges and public prosecutors of the ordinary courts. Furthermore, the members of the commercial and labour courts are not career judges but professionals elected either by members of the trades (commercial courts) or, on the basis of parity, by employees and employers (labour courts). The following text will not deal with the recruitment and training of these judges but with that of the judges and prosecutors of the ordinary courts.

I. Requirements for admission to the professions of judge and public prosecutor and initial training

In France, judges and public prosecutors are primarily recruited by means of three competitive entrance exams to the Legal Service Training College (*Ecole Nationale de la Magistrature*, hereinafter referred to as "ENM") and marginally by way of recruitment on the basis of qualifications.

Each of the three competitive entrance exams to the ENM is judged by an independent jury. The jury for the first two exams - the external and internal exams - is identical. It is composed of a judge "outside of the hierarchy" of the Court of Cassation, as chairman, two university professors or senior lecturers responsible for legal education, a member of the Conseil d'Etat or a judge of the Auditor-General's Department, and a judge or prosecutor of an ordinary court. For certain subjects, however, specialised examiners may be added to the jury.

In order to sit any of the competitive exams, candidates must have French citizenship, enjoy their civil rights and be of good moral standing, be in a lawful position with respect to the laws relating to military service, fulfil the health requirements necessary to exercise the functions and meet certain age requirements.

Depending on the exam taken, the candidates must also meet the following requirements:

- candidates taking the external examination must hold a diploma showing the completion of at least four years of post-secondary education or a diploma judged to be equivalent and must be no older than 27 on the 1st of January of the year of the exam;

- candidates taking the internal exam must be no older than 40 on the 1st of January of the year of the exam, have the status of a civil servant or an employee of the State, a territorial authority, one of their public institutions or of the public hospital service and have served four years in the public service on the 1st of January of the year of the exam;

- finally, candidates taking the third exam must be no older than 40 on the 1st of January of the year of the exam, have eight years of professional experience in the private sector or as an elected member of an assembly, of a territorial authority, or in judicial functions in a non-professional capacity.

The competitive entrance exams for the ENM consist of written tests to determine the admissibility of the candidates and oral exams accompanied by a physical test to determine admission. With respect to the first and second exams, the admissibility tests include an essay on a topic relating to social, legal, economic and cultural aspects of the present day world, an essay on civil law, an essay on criminal or public law, at the candidate's choice, and a synthesis of documents relating to legal problems. Each of these tests lasts five hours.

The admission tests include a 30 minute interview with the jury on a subject relating to social, legal, political, economic and cultural aspects of the present day world or on a commentary of a general text, whichever the candidate chooses; a 15 minute oral examination relating to, at the candidate's choice, a topic of commercial or administrative law; three similar oral examinations relating to the subjects - criminal or public law - not chosen for the written portion, the organisation of the courts and civil, criminal and administrative procedure, and finally, social security law; a test of living language lasting 30 minutes; a test involving physical exercises.

The tests of the third examination are to be determined by a decree currently under preparation.

Each test of the competitive examination is marked from 1 to 20 and bears a certain coefficient. By adding up the results of each of the tests, each jury draws up a list of admissible candidates, then a list of admitted candidates, within the limits of the number of places of study to be filled in the school.

The candidates selected must then undergo a training period in the ENM before being admitted to the office of judge or public prosecutor. During this training period, they have the status of legal trainees and receive remuneration. The training, lasting 31 months, alternates periods of study during which the legal trainees receive theoretical instruction, lead discussions and carry out simulation exercises, with work placements devoted to the observation of an institution or of a professional environment, and to the progressive learning within a court of the practical exercise of judicial functions.

This training period is concluded with the final exams whose results, combined with the marks received during the study period and work placement, rank the students according to merit. The ranking jury may eliminate from the ranking list any students whom, in light of their marks, they consider incapable of carrying out judicial functions. These students are, at the jury's choice, excluded or invited to spend an additional year at the school. The ranked students must, following their ranking, choose their first post as judge or public prosecutor from a list of posts drawn up by the Justice Ministry. On the basis of this choice, the final period of initial training begins which is dedicated to functional specialisation. This specialisation centered on the function chosen by the student, consists of a 5 week period of study at the school, followed by a training period of the same length in a regional court specialising in the function chosen. After this training period, the student is appointed judge/public prosecutor by decree of the President of the Republic, which issued with the approval of the Judicial Service Commission, if it relates to a judge, or on the basis of the Commission's opinion if it relates to a public prosecutor.

Aside from the competitive entrance exams for the ENM, there are two exceptional ways to be admitted to the judiciary or the public prosecution service. The first allows direct access to the ENM as a student. This avenue is open to persons not over 40 years of age, holding at least a master's degree of law and having several years of professional experience qualifying them to exercise judicial functions. The only preliminary selection process consists in the examination of the file by the Commission for the promotion of judicial personnel, which decides on the admission.

The second exceptional way to be admitted as a judge or public prosecutor enables direct access to the profession of a judge or as a member of the prosecution service. Persons who have French citizenship, fulfil the same requirements as to their degree as for the first of the competitive entrance examinations to the ENM and who have seven years of professional experience particularly qualifying them to exercise judicial functions may be candidates for direct integration into the judiciary for the exercise of first or second grade functions. The files of the candidates are submitted to the Commission for the promotion of judicial personnel. Lastly, certain limited categories of persons may be directly appointed to higher functions, so-called "extra-hierarchical" categories. This avenue of access to judicial functions is exceptional and essentially aimed at permitting professors of law or lawyers at the Conseil d'Etat or the Court of Cassation to sit in the latter Court.

II.   Further training of judges and public prosecutors

A "right to further training" for French judges and public prosecutors is recognised in the rules governing the judicial personnel. The ENM is responsible for this training and it annually offers a national training programme, to which it has added since 1989 a mechanism of decentralised further training at the level of the Courts of Appeal. The proposed training activities consist of seminars and internships relating to legal, economic, social and political topics. Bilateral exchanges with foreign judges/public prosecutors are also organised. There are, lastly, training activities reserved for specific persons, namely for judges and public prosecutors having just over one year of experience in their new office, for those changing their functions and for new heads of courts.

Several hundred training activities are organised every year; attendance is strictly voluntary. Each judge/public prosecutor currently is entitled to at least five days of training per year.

III. Reforms likely to be introduced in the near future

An organisational statute, promulgated in January 1995, introduces two innovations concerning the recruitment of judges and public prosecutors. The first of these innovations concerns the possibility of recruiting, until 31 December 1999, judges and deputy public prosecutors of the Court of Appeal on extraordinary service, who will exercise their functions for a non-renewable term of 5 years. The second innovation is the organisation of the recruitment of temporary judges, first on an experimental basis in three Courts of Appeal. The persons recruited in this way will exercise the functions of a small claims court judge or non-presiding judge in the regional court for a non-renewable term of seven years.

Moreover, a draft decree currently being prepared includes certain modifications concerning the competitive entrance exam to the ENM. It lays down the nature of the tests for the third entrance exam and provides for including in the programme of the three competitive exams of European and Community Law, which should be integrated into the programme of the test in public law. The draft lastly provides for an increase of the manpower of the examination juries, to generalise the double marking of the written tests and to implement double questioning in the oral examination.

GERMANY

I. Requirements for admission to the professions of judge and public prosecutor and initial training

In Germany, judges and public prosecutors are not recruited on the basis of a competitive entrance exam, but appointed - or elected - in different manners. Their initial training nevertheless follows an identical path.

To apply for the office of a judge or public prosecutor, applicants must have completed legal studies at a university, followed by the first State exam in law. The following step consists of a legal preparatory service lasting two years; this training is not aimed solely at the profession of judge but at all legal professions. This preparatory service includes training periods with civil and criminal courts, with a public prosecutor, an administrative authority and a lawyer. The training period is concluded by the second State exam in law. Persons successful in this exam may then apply for a post of judge or public prosecutor.

In most cases, recruitment of new judges/public prosecutors takes place directly after the second State exam - above average examination results are required - but professional experience in the legal field is always appreciated.

The modes of appointment of judges and public prosecutors vary according to whether they are called to exercise their functions at the federal or *Länder* level. Thus judges at the Federal Constitutional Court are elected one half by the Federal Council (*Bundesrat*) and by an election committee consisting of twelve members of the Federal Parliament (*Bundestag*), by a majority of two-thirds, and then appointed by the Federal President. The judges of the highest federal courts are appointed by the Federal Committee for the selection of judges and by the competent federal minister. They are first selected by the Council responsible for judicial appointments (*Präsidialrat*), after which the competent minister decides whether to appoint them himself or to ask the Federal President to do so. Lastly, other federal judges are appointed by the Federal President upon the proposal of the competent federal minister.

The vast majority of judges (approximately 97%) are however in the service of the *Länder*. These judges are either jointly appointed by a committee for the selection of judges and by the Justice Minister of the *Land*, or appointed by the latter alone.

Finally, public prosecutors are appointed by the Justice Minister of the *Land* in which they are called to exercise their profession or by the Federal Justice Minister for the small number exercising their profession at the federal level.

II. Further training of judges and public prosecutors

In Germany, possibilities of further training for judges and public prosecutors exist at both the federal and *Länder* level.

At the federal level, further training, for whose organisation the federal Justice Minister is reponsible, takes place under the aegis of the German Academy of Judges (*Deutsche Richterakademie*). This institution offers judges and public prosecutors courses permitting them not only to accentuate their specialisation but also to inform themselves on general socio-political and economic problems. Approximately 100 one week training programmes are organised each year by the Academy.

At the *Länder* level, numerous training activities are organised by the Justice Ministers. They have more or less the same content as those existing at the federal level, but they also include courses specifically aimed at judges or public prosecutors with little experience.

Participation in all these training activities is voluntary.

III. Reforms likely to be introduced in the near future

In Germany, no reforms are currently planned in the areas of recruitment and training of judges and public prosecutors.

GREECE

I. **Requirements for admission to the professions of judge and public prosecutor and initial training**

In Greece, admission to the professions of judge and public prosecutor is based exclusively on a competitive entrance exam. The body responsible for the selection is the National School of Judicial Service. The candidate must have a bachelors degree of law and be between 25 and 32 years old. However, exceptions to the higher age limit exist for candidates having done their military service, doctors of law, who are allowed to sit the exam until the age of 35, and those having a diploma higher than the bachelor's degree of law who may be up to 33 years old.

The exam is made up of two parts: the first determines admissibility to the National School of Judicial Service; and the second, admission. The admissibility exams consist of written exams on the following subjects: constitutional and administrative law, civil and commercial law, criminal law, general education and a written exam on a subject the student may choose from among the subjects of community law, tax law, or labour law. The part of the examination determining admission consists of written synthesis exams on practical questions concerning constitutional, administrative and public international law, commercial and civil law as well as one of the optional subjects not chosen for the written admissibility exams. It also includes oral examinations relating to constitutional and administrative law, civil and commercial law, criminal law, civil, criminal and administrative procedure, and on the optional subjects of the admissibility exam. An exam in a foreign language is also provided for on an optional basis. Finally, the notice of the examination may provide for the presentation by the candidate of a file for the purpose of assessing his abilities for analysis and synthesis.

The candidates admitted then undergo theoretical and practical training at the National School of Judicial Service lasting from 32 to 36 months. The theoretical training includes attendance of conferences and seminars and drawing up files, commentaries of texts and essays. Not only purely legal subjects are dealt with, but also others topics such as psychology, sociology, economics, computer science or history. The practical training is made up of training periods in different institutions: courts, public services, banks, international organisations ...

The legal trainees are subjected to further controls of their knowledge during and after the period of training. When they leave the school, they are appointed judges or public prosecutors for a trial period of six months.

II. Further training of judges and public prosecutors

The possibility of undergoing further training is granted in theory to judges and public prosecutors by a law of 1994, but the implementing decrees of this law fixing the means of putting into place the requisite training activities have not yet been promulgated.

III. Reforms likely to be introduced in the near future

No reform in this area is currently on the agenda in Greece.

HUNGARY

I. Requirements for admission to the professions of judge and public prosecutor and initial training

In Hungary, admission to the professions of judge and public prosecutor is not based on competitive examinations, but on appointments: judges are appointed for life by the President of the Republic upon proposal by the Justice Minister, who bases himself on the proposal made to him by the president of the county court in which a post is vacant. As far as public prosecutors are concerned, they are appointed for life by the Prosecutor General of the Republic of Hungary. The latter is not appointed, but elected by Parliament upon proposal by the President of the Republic.

The requirements to be met by the candidates for the office of judge or public prosecutor are similar: they must be at least 24 years old, have no criminal record, have completed their studies of law at the university and have passed a professional examination. Candidates for the office of public prosecutor must in addition have had at least two years of legal practice.

There is no training following the appointment; the preparation of the professional exam is considered to constitute sufficient training. Nevertheless, the presidents of the county courts provide preparation for this examination for the benefit of the candidates doing an internship in their courts.

II. Further training of judges and public prosecutors

Hungarian judges and public prosecutors have the possibility of further training in the course of their careers. It is organised for judges by the Directorate of improvement and further training of the Justice Ministry; for public prosecutors, it is organised by the Directorate of further training and human resources of the Supreme Prosecutor's Office.

The topics dealt with in these training activities are not the same for judges and public prosecutors. For judges, the topics depend on the problems encountered by the courts; a training schedule, countersigned by the presidents of the county courts, is drawn up annually. Some topics which are not purely legal are sometimes also included in the training schedule, such as, for example, ethics of the courts, psychological knowledge related to the work of judges or foreign legal terminology.

In the training activities reserved for public prosecutors, the topics most often dealt with include rhetoric (this is especially aimed at public prosecutors at the start of their careers), communication, sociology (for prosecutors dealing with matters concerning minors), psychology and criminology.

In 1994, 24 conferences, seminars and various courses were held for judges and nine courses intended for public prosecutors. Attendance in these activities is mandatory for judges or public prosecutors designated by their superiors.

III. Reforms likely to be introduced in the near future

In Hungary, no reforms are currently in progress or planned concerning the admission or training of judges and public prosecutors.

ITALY

I. Requirements for admission to the professions of judge and public prosecutor and initial training

In Italy, admission to the professions of judge and public prosecutor is based solely on a competitive examination. This exam, which is the same for both professions, is organised by a commission appointed by the Judicial Service Commission and made up of judges/public prosecutors and university professors. The requirements are that the candidates must have Italian citizenship, enjoy their civil rights, be of good moral standing and hold a master's degree in law. Moreover, at the date of the notice of the examination, they must be between 21 and 35 years old.

The examination consists of written papers in civil law, criminal law and administrative law which determine admissibility, and oral exams relating to Roman law, civil, criminal, administrative and constitutional law, criminal and civil procedure, labour law, the law of the relationship between the State and the Catholic Church, international law and statistics: these oral exams determine the admission of the candidates.

The candidates admitted on the basis of the examination take on the functions of judge/public prosecutor, with a status as legal trainees, and must then undergo a two year training period, which is identical for judges and public prosecutors. It is moreover possible in Italy to move at any given time from one profession to another. The organisation of this training is the responsibility of the Judicial Service Commission which in turn relies on the Judicial Councils elected by the judges of each Court of Appeal.

The initial training of judges/public prosecutors, lasting one year, includes theoretical courses and practical training periods in the courts. At the end of one year of training and with the favourable opinion of the Judicial Council, they may be appointed deputy public prosecutors or be assigned to a "pretura" (first instance court composed of one judge).

Once the training period has been completed, the legal trainee, with the approval of the competent Judicial Council and after the deliberation of the Judicial Service Commission, is appointed to a post of judge/public prosecutor, subject to the condition that he has effectively exercised judicial functions for not less than one year. Legal trainees to whom the Judicial Service Commission has not assigned a post must prolong their training period for two additional years, at the end of which they are assessed again according to the same procedure. The trainee who is twice found to be unsuitable for fulfilling judicial functions is excluded.

II. Further training of judges and public prosecutors

Within the framework of further education, the Judicial Service Commission organises meetings and study seminars of judges/public prosecutors to facilitate their staying up to date professionally. The subjects dealt with are topical themes concerning not only civil, criminal and administrative law but also community and international law. Each year approximately ten training activities are organised, each of which is attended by approximately one hundred judges/public prosecutors. Attendance is voluntary, and it is the Judicial Service Commission which chooses the participants of each meeting or seminar. Once admitted, however, the judge/public prosecutor must, except for any last minute inability to do so, attend the event for which he is registered.

Other training activities also exist parallel to those organised by the Judicial Service Commission. The Justice Ministry also organises courses in foreign languages for which interested judges/public prosecutors may apply.

Finally, the Presidency of the Court of Cassation, acting in conjunction with the Presidency of the Bar Association of Rome and the professors of the Faculty of Law of this city, organise every year seven seminars concerning legal problems relating to divergences between doctrine and case-law. These seminars are open to all those wishing to attend.

III. Reforms likely to be introduced in the near future

The reform of the basic law relating to the organisation of the courts has been under study for some time. Recently, the Justice Minister, in an official meeting with the members of the Judicial Service Commission examined the advisability of requiring candidates for the competitive entrance exam for the professions of judge and public prosecutor to have a more extensive general education, covering areas other than law, in order to permit them to better fulfil their future functions.

Other changes are also proposed at regular intervals but have not yet lead to any reform proposal. Thus, one often speaks of establishing a Judicial Service Training College; recently, political circles have raised the question of the separation of the careers of judge and public prosecutor, but this has met with great opposition from the judges and public prosecutors.

LATVIA

I. Requirements for admission to the professions of judge and public prosecutor and initial training

In Latvia, there are no competitive entrance exams to the professions of judge or public prosecutor; these offices are filled by means of appointment.

The requirements to be met by the candidates for these offices are to have Latvian citizenship and to have completed higher legal studies. Candidates are furthermore required to have, depending on the post applied for, two to four years of professional legal experience. Finally, the minimum age for judges of first instance courts is 25 years and of the administrative court, 23 years.

Judges and public prosecutors are appointed at first for a trial period of six months to two years for judges and one month to one year for public prosecutors. Afterwards, they must sit a qualification exam organised on the basis of a procedure established by the Justice Minister. The bodies responsible for the assessment are, for judges, the Committee for the examination of judicial competence, and for public prosecutors, the examination commission appointed by the Prosecutor General.

After having served the trial period and passed the professional qualification exam, judges and public prosecutors are permanently appointed; the former, by the Justice Minister - with the exception of the judges of the first instance courts who are appointed by Parliament upon the recommendation of the Justice Minister - and the latter, by the Prosecutor General. The Prosecutor General is elected for seven years by Parliament.

II. Further training of judges and public prosecutors

There are possibilities of further training for judges and public prosecutors, respectively organised by the Centre for Information and Training of Judges and by the Department of Methodology of the Prosecutor General's Office.

The Centre for Information and Training of Judges offers training activities relating to questions of law and judicial practice which are aimed at both new and experienced judges. A training committee was established to evaluate more precisely the training needs and to draw up an annual training schedule to respond to these needs. This Committee has recently proposed setting up courses and conferences relating to ethics, psychology and other non-legal disciplines useful in the activities of judges.

Further training of prosecutors is only in its beginning stages - the public prosecution service of Latvia has only been recently set up - but is currently undergoing continuous development. Further training consists of one day seminars relating to new laws and practical problems encountered by prosecutors in their activities; one or two week courses reserved for prosecutors promoted to new functions, as well as other one week courses adapted to the needs of each category of prosecutors (experienced prosecutors, heads of prosecution, prosecutors specialising in a particular field). From time to time, these courses are offered in non-legal disciplines such as foreign languages and accounting.

III. Reforms likely to be introduced in the near future

No reform is currently envisaged in Latvia as the present laws on the organisation of the courts have only recently entered into force - 1 January 1993 for the Law on the judiciary and 1 July 1994 for the Law on the prosecution service. However, in the medium term, it is possible that the trial periods of judges and prosecutors will be harmonised.

LITHUANIA

I. Requirements for admission to the professions of judge and public prosecutor and initial training

In Lithuania, the means of admission to the professions of judge and public prosecutor are different; the former must pass a recruitment exam, whereas the latter need not.

A. *Admission to the profession of judge*

The selection of candidates for the profession of judge is carried out by two distinct bodies. The Judicial Examination Commission of Lithuanian Courts, composed of the President of the Supreme Court and the Justice Minister, with a mandate of three years, is responsible for the selection of candidates for the profession of judge. The Examination Commission of the Supreme Court, composed of five members appointed for three years by the Judges' Council, is responsible for the examination of candidacies for the post of judge of the Supreme Court.

The requirements for candidates for the office of judge vary with the post they wish to fill. Candidates for local courts must be at least 25 years old on the day of their appointment, have an irreproachable reputation, have received university education in law and have two years of professional legal experience. Finally, they must also pass the recruitment exam for judges of local courts.

Candidates for a post of judge of the Court of Appeal or of the District Court must fulfil the same requirements stated above and have not less than five years of professional experience as a judge, public prosecutor, barrister or arbitrator, and must have passed the exam for the post in question.

Finally, candidates may be appointed to a post as judge of the Supreme Court if they have ten years experience with a court of appeal or district court or if they have a doctorate in law. Here also, a special recruitment examination is foreseen.

These requirements are the only ones which must be met by candidates for the office of judge. The persons chosen access directly and permanently the office of judge. However, judges of local courts are invited, within five months after their appointment, to participate in a specific one month training programme. This programme, organised by the Justice Ministry, is however not mandatory except for judges having less than ten years professional legal experience.

Judges at the beginning of their careers are not subject to any limitations with respect to the functions which they may exercise, except one: in practice, judges of local courts may not be less than 25 years of age; judges under 25 years of age may only hear certain matters, namely administrative law matters, those relating to maintenance questions, and non-contentious civil cases reserved to them by law.

It should be noted that the above-mentioned procedure is the only avenue of admission to the profession of judge.

B. *Admission to the profession of public prosecutor*

Contrary to judges, public prosecutors need not sit a recruitment exam. They are directly appointed by the Prosecutor General from among the candidates fulfilling the following requirements: have Lithuanian citizenship, have studied law and have an irreproachable reputation. The Prosecutor General and his deputies must be at least 30 years old and have had at least ten years of experience as a judge, prosecutor or investigator. Finally, from a certain rank of the hierarchy upwards, prosecutors must have at least three years of experience in the offices mentioned above. Persons not meeting these experience requirements but nevertheless selected must work as public servants for one year. The Law on the prosecution service also provides that the Prosecutor General's Office must establish a specific training programme.

II. Further training of judges and public prosecutors

Today, there is no system of further training for judges and public prosecutors in Lithuania even though such a system existed in the former Socialist Republic of Lithuania. The greatest obstacle to its establishment is the lack of persons qualified to offer such training.

III. Reforms likely to be introduced in the near future

The present Law on the organisation of the courts entered into effect on 1 January 1995; no reforms are envisaged in the near future.

LUXEMBOURG

I. Requirements for admission to the professions of judge and public prosecutor and initial training

Luxembourg has neither a competitive entrance examination nor a recruitment test for admission to the offices of judge or public prosecutor.

After having completed their basic law studies (masters degree in law or equivalent), persons wishing to become judges must complete a three year judicial training period consisting of a theoretical instruction portion and a practical portion during which the candidate works either as trainee lawyer under a principal who is a barrister or as a trainee judicial assistant attached to the judiciary.

At the end of the judicial training period, candidates are required to sit an end of training examination, which they must pass in order to be admitted to the professions of judge and prosecutor. The candidates are then appointed to the office of judicial assistants by the Justice Minister on the basis of an opinion of the State Prosecutor General.

For their selection, these authorities primarily rely on the ranking of the candidate in the final examination as well as on the assessment of his professional performance during his practical training period.

The candidates recruited in this way must then complete one year of training within the judiciary before their final appointment to a particular post of judge or prosecutor. This training period permits the initiation of the new judges and prosecutors to professional practice; it is completed by theoretical training focusing in particular on English legal terminology, accounting, drafting of judgments, ethics and basic computer skills.

II. Further training of judges and public prosecutors

Further training for judges and public prosecutors is not compulsory in Luxembourg, and there is no specific framework for such training.

The Justice Minister may however authorise on an ad hoc basis judges or public prosecutors to take courses which are useful for the practice of their profession.

III. Reforms likely to be introduced in the near future

No reforms relating to admission to judicial careers or the training of judges or public prosecutors are currently envisaged in Luxembourg.

MOLDOVA

I. Requirements for admission to the professions of judge and public prosecutor and initial training

In Moldova, judges and public prosecutors are recruited on the basis of a selection test which, for the former, consists of an examination and for the latter, an interview. There is no other means of access to these professions.

The body responsible for the selection of judges is the Justice Ministry; public prosecutors are chosen by the Principal State Counsel's Office.

In order to be admitted to judicial functions, candidates must have Moldavian citizenship and have completed higher legal studies. Those wishing to become judges must moreover be at least 25 years old and have two years of legal experience.

The candidates which are selected must then undergo a training period of one year with a court or state counsel's office, depending on the profession they intend to enter. However, for judges, this training period is only mandatory when the persons recruited do not have the requisite professional experience. When they do have such experience, they are directly elected to a post by Parliament, upon joint proposal by the Justice Minister and the President of the Supreme Court of Justice.

II. Further training of judges and public prosecutors

Judges and public prosecutors have access to further training which is organised by the Justice Ministry for judges and by the the Principal State Counsel's Office for public prosecutors. The training activities offered, eight per year for judges and twelve per year for public prosecutors, consist of courses and seminars, attendance of which is mandatory.

III. Reforms likely to be introduced in the near future

Parliament has just voted in the first reading a draft law relating to the organisation of the courts and the status of judges.

THE NETHERLANDS

I. Requirements for admission to the professions of judge and public prosecutor and initial training

Persons under 30 years of age who wish to enter the professions of judge or public prosecutor are recruited on the basis of a different procedure from that applied to persons who are older. In practice, those belonging to the first category undergo a selective recruitment test, while the others are selected on an individual basis rather than after a competitive examination.

The body responsible for the organisation of the selective recruitment test is a committee composed of three representatives of the judiciary, another of the Justice Ministry and one representative of the civil society. Applicants for this exam must have Dutch nationality, be under the age of 30 years, have a university law degree and produce a formal statement of good behaviour.

The recruitment test is composed of two parts. The first selection is carried out on the basis of a test assessing the analytical ability and intelligence of the candidates. The final selection is made on the basis of a psychological test, personal interviews and references.

The persons selected on the basis of these tests then undergo a six year training period, followed by one or two years of probationary admission to judicial functions, after which they are permanently admitted to the profession they have chosen.

Persons who are older than 30 and have six years of professional experience preparing them to perform judicial functions, do not need to take the recruitment test. They may apply directly with the court or the public prosecutor's department they wish to enter. A special committee is responsible for evaluating the admissibility of the applicant, and the decision on his admission is made by the court.

The body responsible for the training of judges and public prosecutors recruited on the basis of the selection examination is the SSR (*Stichting Studiecentrum Rechtspleging*), ie the independent foundation for the study and training of the judiciary. This training consists of practical training periods with the courts and public prosecutor's departments and theoretical courses. During this period, the candidates generally spend 26 months in a court, 10 months in a public prosecutor's department and 12 additional months in one of these two institutions at the candidate's choice and 24 months in a law firm. At the end of each training period, the student's skills, qualifications and performance in the professional environment are assessed.

Judges or public prosecutors recruited on an individual basis have an "à la carte" training programme. The SSR is only responsible for the theoretical courses; the organisation of the practical training is the responsibility of the court or public prosecutor's department to which the new recruit belongs.

II. Further training of judges and public prosecutors

Dutch judges and public prosecutors have the opportunity, during their careers, to participate in different activities of further training organised by the SSR. The courses offered, approximately 150 per year attracting over 6,000 participants, relate to, inter alia, communication, social skills in court and management. Participation in these courses is voluntary.

III. Reforms likely to be introduced in the near future

Currently under discussion in the Netherlands is the appropriateness of the common training programme for young judges and public prosecutors. Some consider it better to have a separate training programme for each of the professions. At the moment, however, the proponents of this change have not yet prevailed.

NORWAY

Judges and public prosecutors are appointed by the government on the basis of a recommendation of the Justice Ministry. Assistant judges are appointed by the Justice Ministry or the courts themselves.

The candidates for the office of judge must meet the following requirements: have Norwegian nationality, be a reliable and trustworthy person and have no criminal record. The judges of the Supreme Court must be at least 30 years old and have obtained the highest mark in the final university examination. Judges of the first and second instances must be at least 25 years old and have obtained the second highest mark in the final university examination.

To be a candidate for the profession of public prosecutor, it is enough to be a trained lawyer.

For judges as well as public prosecutors, the Justice Ministry relies on, in its choice of candidates, the marks obtained in the final university examination and professional experience, in particular in the legal field. Experience with the Justice Ministry, a university or a law firm is especially sought.

Once appointed, judges and public prosecutors need not undergo any particular training. Moreover, Norwegian legislation does not provide for any possibility of further training.

No reform of the current system of recruitment of judges and public prosecutors is on the agenda in Norway.

POLAND

I. Requirements for admission to the professions of judge and public prosecutor and initial training

In Poland, admission to the professions of judge and public prosecutor is based on a competitive entrance exam. This exam is organised for judges by the Presidents of the provincial courts and the courts of appeal; and for public prosecutors, by the chief prosecutors attached to these tribunals. The requirements to be met by the candidates are the same for both professions: ie Polish nationality, the enjoyment of civil and political rights, a high moral standing and a university degree in law.

The tests of the competitive exam are also the same for both professions. They include tests relating to all branches of the law and/or an essay on one of several proposed topics. Aside from the legal knowledge of the candidates, their written and oral ability to express their thoughts is given special consideration. The competitive entrance examination does not yet include psychological tests but it is intended to introduce them, perhaps in the near future.

At the end of this competitive entrance exam, the candidates are selected on the basis of their files and the results obtained in the selection tests.

Once selected, the candidates are not directly admitted to the office of judge or public prosecutor, but must undergo a two year training period, at the end of which they must pass one of the state exams prior to the admission to the office of judge or public prosecutor - a specific exam for each of the two professions.

The above-mentioned training period is organised by the training division in the personnel department of the Justice Ministry, and by the training units of the provincial courts or appeal courts and their respective public prosecutor's offices. The training programme is established by the Ministry, while the courts are responsible for its practical organisation. This training period consists of seminars relating to criminal and civil law and of internships of varying lengths with all the different kinds of courts. The trainee judges and prosecutors have the status of public servants during this period of training.

At the end of this training period, the students are assessed on the basis of their results in the partial examination - which is held at the end of the first year of training - and in the final examination, and on the basis of the opinions of the persons responsible for their various internships.

Even though the competitive entrance examination is the normal avenue of admission to the profession of judge or public prosecutor, it is possible for some legal professionals to enter these professions without sitting the examination: ie, university professors or those of their collaborators having the title of "*doktor habilitowany*" or a higher title, and barristers and solicitors specialised in commercial law. There is also a "bridge" between the professions of judge and public prosecutor, as prosecutors who have practised for three years may be admitted to the profession of judge; judges may themselves be admitted to the profession of public prosecutor without meeting this requirement. These persons must however be appointed to their new offices according to the normal procedure requiring opinions of the persons concerned. Once recruited, they need not undergo any special training.

II. Further training of judges and public prosecutors

Further training of judges and public prosecutors is organised, like their initial training, by the training division in the personnel department of the Justice Ministry and the training units attached to the various provincial courts or courts of apppeal and their respective public prosecutor's offices. The training division of the Justice Ministry is responsible for organising training activities at a national level, while the courts deal only with the training of judges and prosecutors working within the jurisdiction of each court.

There is no pre-established programme of further training. Such training consists of conferences, seminars, and workshops relating mainly, but not exclusively, to legal matters. In respect of training organised at a regional level, topics are suggested by court presidents.

In 1994, 12 conferences were organised by the Justice Ministry, attended by 960 judges and public prosecutors; at the regional level, 34 conferences aimed at judges and 49 conferences aimed at public prosecutors took place, attracting respectively 2,500 and 3,000 persons. These figures do not include the conferences organised by the judicial associations, private foundations and other similar bodies. Attendance is voluntary; the interested persons must however obtain the approval of their superior.

III. Reforms likely to be introduced in the near future

Some reforms relating to the training of judges and public prosecutors are currently under study in Poland. In particular, the extension of the training period to three years instead of two is foreseen, as well as the changing of this training programme and the adoption of a two-tier training scheme with practitioners trained at the national level becoming teachers at the regional level.

PORTUGAL

I. Requirements for admission to the professions of judge and public prosecutor and initial training

In Portugal, lawyers who wish to enter the professions of judge and public prosecutor must be admitted to the Centre of Judicial Studies where they undergo the training necessary for practising these professions. This is the only means of admission to these professions.

Admission to the Centre of Judicial Studies is done on the basis of a competitive exam organised by the Centre consisting of a written and an oral phase. Persons holding a degree of doctor of law are exempted from this exam. Some persons are exempted from having to sit the written exams: these are barristers having seven years of professional experience and receiving a favourable recommendation from the Bar; registrars and notaries, also having seven years of experience and who have obtained the mark "good" or higher from their superiors; and legal officers with bachelor's degrees in law provided that they have ten years experience and have received the mark of "very good". Finally, persons having a bachelor's degree in law having exercised for seven years the functions of a staff member of the public prosecutor's office without being public prosecutors and who have received the evaluation of "Good" for at least five years are exempted from the competitive exam for entrance into the special training course for public prosecutors.

To be admitted to the Centre of Judicial Studies, the candidates must fulfil the following requirements: have Portuguese nationality, a bachelor's degree of law from a Portuguese university or a foreign diploma recognised as being equivalent, be more than 23 years old, enjoy their civil and political rights and fulfil all other requirements for admission into the civil service.

As already mentioned, the competitive entrance exam to the centre consists of two phases. The written phase includes the following tests: an essay relating to social, economic or cultural topics, a practical case in civil and commercial law and civil procedure, a practical case in criminal law and criminal procedure and a synthesis based on documents relating to legal problems.

The oral phase includes: a discussion relating to legal, ethical and cultural topics chosen from a previously published list, a discussion relating to the subjects of the written tests and questioning relating to a legal topic drawn by lot from a list of previously published topics.

There are no precise criteria for the evaluation of candidates; the law limits itself to establishing that they are assessed by a jury composed of the director and professors of the Centre, judges appointed by the Judicial Service Commission and some eminent persons in the cultural field.

The selected candidates must undergo a training period organised by the Centre of Judicial Studies. This period is made up of three stages: a theoretical and practical training period lasting six months, a training period of initiation of the same duration and a pre-posting training period of eight and one half months.

The theoretical and practical training period is made up of courses on three kinds of subjects: training subjects such as legal methodology, legal psychology, foreign languages; professional and applied subjects, among which are found case-law analysis, criminology and forensic medicine; finally, the informative and specialisation subjects, such as comparative law, organisation of the courts and business administration.

At the end of this period, the candidates are graded; those having received a grade of "insufficient" are excluded, while those having received the grades of "good" and "sufficient" may continue to the following phase.

The subsequent phase consists of an initiation training period in the courts under the direction of, depending on the case, a judge or a public prosecutor. During this period, the trainee judges participate in judicial tasks under the responsibility of an instructing judge or prosecutor and in additional activities of training and of transition between the theoretical period and the pre-posting training period. At the end of this initiation training period, the trainees are once again assessed and those found to be unsatisfactory are excluded. The others are ranked according to various criteria including the marks received during the training period, the results of the competitive entrance exam and the academic programme. The trainee judges are then appointed by the Judicial Service Commission or by the Superior Council of the Prosecutor's Office to a post of judge or delegate of the Attorney-General of the Republic in a trainee capacity.

They then move on to the third and last phase of the initial training which is the pre-posting training period during which they perform their functions under their personal responsibility but with the assistance of experienced judges/public prosecutors.

During the training period, trainee judges have the status of a junior legal officer and are subjected to the rights, duties and incompatibilities of civil servants; they receive remuneration equal to half of that alloted to judges and delegates of the public prosecutor. Trainees who are civil servants or employees of the State, however, may receive the remuneration applicable to their original professional category.

During the pre-posting training period, the trainees are subject to the same rights, duties and incompatibilities as judges/public prosecutors and receive the same remuneration.

II. Further training of judges and public prosecutors

During their careers, Portuguese judges and public prosecutors have the opportunity to undergo further training organised by the Centre of Judicial Studies. Two kinds of training activities exist: the first are aimed at newly-appointed judges and public prosecutors. They consist of various complementary training activities which are mandatory for them during the first five years of service. These courses extend over periods which must not exceed one month per year and three months in total.

Moreover, the Centre of Judicial Studies annually organises study sessions, seminars, colloqia and other similiar activities designed to provide information, updating of knowledge and perfecting of the training of all judges and public prosecutors. Attendance in these activities is purely voluntary.

III. Reforms likely to be introduced in the near future

There are no reforms currently in progress or envisaged in Portugal relating to the admission to and training in the professions of judge and public prosecutor.

ROMANIA

I. Requirements for admission to the professions of judge and public prosecutor and initial training

The normal admission procedure for the professions of judge and public prosecutor provides for neither a competitive entrance examination nor a recruitment test. Judges and public prosecutors are, with the exception of trainees, appointed by decree of the President of the Republic on proposal of the Judicial Service Commission. As far as trainee judges and prosecutors are concerned, they are appointed by the Justice Minister and may only act in the first instance courts and prosecutor's offices.

The requirements for admission as judges/public prosecutors are the following: have Romanian citizenship, reside in Romania and possess all civil rights, have a bachelor's degree in law, have completed the internship prescribed by law, have no criminal record and a good reputation, speak the Romanian language and finally be judged to be physically suitable for the office of judge or public prosecutor.

However, the Romanian legal system is still in a period of transition, and professional tests are periodically organised for admission to the professions of judge and prosecutor for persons coming from other legal professions and meeting the general requirements of admission to the judiciary/prosecution.

For candidates for the office of judge, the recruitment tests are organised by the Justice Ministry; for candidates for the office of public prosecutor, the body responsible for the selection is the prosecution service. These tests, which are the same for both professions, includes tests in civil law, criminal law, civil procedure, criminal procedure and commercial law, graded from one to ten.

The candidates selected at the end of this recruitment test are admitted directly to the office of judge or public prosecutor subject to having a certain seniority in the previously practised legal profession and to having passed the qualification exam required by law. The candidates not meeting these requirements are appointed on a trial basis to the status of trainee judge/public prosecutor and, at the end of two years of training, must take the qualification exam.

Voluntary initial training is provided for trainee judges and public prosecutors. This training, offered by the National Institute for the Training of Judges/Public Prosecutors lasts nine months, and its purpose is to teach judges/public prosecutors at the beginning of their careers the practical skills required for the practice of their profession and in particular the procedural skills. During these nine months, trainee judges/public prosecutors take two days of courses per week at the Justice Ministry; these courses include working on files, practical cases, simulations and individual work putting the emphasis mostly on criminology, legal reasoning and legal psychology. During the other three days, the trainee judges/public prosecutors do their training in the courts of Bucarest, each of them being supervised by a judge or expert public prosecutor appointed by the Institute.

II. Further training of judges and public prosecutors

Judges and public prosecutors have, during their career, the possibility of undergoing continued training. For judges, this is organised by the Directorate of organisation and personnel of the Justice Ministry; for public prosecutors, by the Section of organisation, studies and control of the Prosecutor's Office. The National Institute for the training of judges/public prosecutors also participates, since its creation in 1992, in the organisation of training activities.

Within the framework of these training activities, one week seminars are organised on specific legal topics, three to four day colloquia for discussion of professional practice and legislative activities, and workshops designed to promote exchanges between judges/public prosecutors on the one hand, and contacts between them and other legal professionals on the other. These training activities number approximately 15 per year for judges and 12 per year for public prosecutors.

There are also other training activities in each court and public prosecutor's office.

Under Article 91 of the Law on the organisation of the courts, judges/public prosecutors are required to periodically undergo continued education activities, in accordance with a programme approved by the Justice Minister.

III. Reforms likely to be introduced in the near future

Some reforms of the area are currently being studied in Romania. It is in particular envisaged that the legal status of the National Institute for the training of judges and public prosecutors will be strengthened by giving it full competence to provide the initial training of judges and prosecutors and to participate in further training.

It is also foreseen to take into account the period of initial training undergone as the case may be by the trainee judges/prosecutors and to deduct its duration from the normal length of the training period.

RUSSIAN FEDERATION

Preliminary remark:

The answers given by the Russian Federation on the questionnaire relate only to the admission to the office of judge.

*
* *

In the Russian Federation, judges are selected on the basis of a recruitment test.

Candidates must meet the following requirements: have a good reputation, have completed university studies in law, and fulfil certain age and seniority requirements: in effect, judges of the first instance courts must be 25 years of age; those of the higher courts must be at least 30 years old and have 5 years of experience in judicial functions; and judges of the Supreme Court must be at least 35 years old and have at least ten years of experience in the exercise of a judicial office.

To be admitted to the office of judge, the candidates must pass a qualification exam before a commission of examiners under the responsibility of a judicial body. Then, they must apply to the qualification board for a recommendation for the office of judge. It is up to the presidents of the courts concerned to put forward the candidacies for the election of judges.

The procedures for appointing judges to district and regional courts as well as to the Supreme Court have not been definitively laid down by legislation. Currently, it is the President of the Federation who appoints the judges to the district, regional courts and courts of the equivalent level; the Federal Council appoints the judges of the Supreme Court.

As a general rule, the law does not limit the judges' term of office; however, judges of the district court are, in practice, at first elected for five years, and then they can be re-elected without limitation on the duration of their term of office.

SLOVAKIA

I. Requirements for admission to the professions of judge and public prosecutor and initial training

It should be pointed out straigh away that public prosecutors in Slovakia are separate from judges and their recruitment and training is organised independently.

There is neither a competitive examination nor a recruitment test prior to admission to the professions of judge or public prosecutor. Persons holding degrees in law wishing to enter one of these professions must apply to a tribunal or to one of the four regional prosecutor's offices and are then invited to an interview.

In the case of judges, the files are examined and the candidates are heard by a committee made up of a regional court judge, a represenative of the Justice Ministry and a member of the Slovak Association of Judges. This committee may, if it finds it necessary, submit the candidates to psychological testing. The persons chosen by the committee become judicial candidates.

The files of the candidates for the office of public prosecutor are examined by a regional public prosecutor. The latter also invites them to an interview and may also require them to undergo psychological testing. He then recommends the proposed candidates to the Prosecutor General who grants them a two year employment contract.

The judicial candidates and trainee public prosecutors must then undergo a training period which ends with compulsory examinations. This training period, lasting two years for public prosecutors and three years for judges, is made up of theoretical and practical training.

Trainees who have completed this training period and who have passed the final exams may then access the offices of judge or public prosecutor. Judges, who must be at least 25 years old, are appointed by the National Council (Parliament) of the Republic, at first for four years, and then, for life. Public prosecutors are appointed for life by the Prosecutor General, subject to the condition that they are at least 24 years old and do not belong to any political party.

II. Further training of judges and public prosecutors

Slovak judges and public prosecutors have access, during their careers, to various possibilities of further training. This training is the responsibility of the Justice Minister for judges and of the Prosecutor General for the prosecution service. The further training activities offered include courses - relating not only to legal topics but also to other disciplines, such as psychology, ethics or foreign languages - seminars and international exchanges. Judges and public prosecutors may also take advantage of various graduate university programmes.

As for the training of judges, it is also necessary to emphasise the role of the Justice Ministry's Law Institute, an independent organisation which is responsible, inter alia, for the organisation of courses, seminars and conferences intended for judges.

III. Reforms likely to be introduced in the near future

A reform concerning the training of public prosecutors is currently being drawn up, but its introduction, which was supposed to take place on 1 May 1995, has been postponed. The main points of this reform concern the establishment of special training for public prosecutors at the beginning of their careers, the creation of an institution specifically responsible for the training of new public prosecutors and the candidates for this office, and the encouragement of participation in graduate training offered by law faculties.

SLOVENIA

I. Requirements for admission to the professions of judge and public prosecutor and initial training

In Slovenia, there is neither a competitive entrance exam nor a recruitment test on which admission to the professions of judge and public prosecutor depends. Judges are appointed for life by the National Assembly upon proposal of the Judicial Service Commission; public prosecutors are also appointed for life, by the government upon proposal of the Justice Minister. The Prosecutor General is elected for six years by the National Assembly upon proposal of the government.

The requirements for entering the professions of judge and public prosecutor are the same: they must be citizens of Slovenia, speak the national language, be in good health, have business skills, be thirty years of age, have a diploma showing the completion of law studies in a Slovene university or a foreign diploma judged to be equivalent; finally, have passed the requisite State exam for the practice of the profession of judge/public prosecutor and be judged suitable to fulfil these functions.

Slovene legislation provides for a single exam required for the practice of the professions of judge, barrister, public prosecutor and notary. A two year training period is organised for the preparation of this exam.

All persons meeting the above-mentioned requirements may apply to undergo this training period. If there are more candidates than available places, the candidates are ranked according to the results they have obtained in their studies.

The training consists of theoretical courses and the following internships:

- four months in a criminal court;

- four months in a civil court;

- two months in a commercial tribunal;

- two months in a labour court.

These internships are mandatory and lead to an assessment of trainees in the form of a written opinion by the persons responsible for their supervision.

At the end of this training period, the trainees apply to write the State exam. They are admitted to this exam is by the Justice Minister, and the exam takes place before a six-member commission. This Commission verifies whether the candidate has acquired all the requisite theoretical knowledge and whether he is qualified to hold the office of judge, public prosecutor, or exercise any other profession for which the law requires the passing of the State exam.

The exam consists of a written phase and an oral phase. The written phase is made up of a test in civil law and a test in criminal law, each lasting eight hours. Upon application of the candidate, one of these two subjects may be replaced by one of his choice. Admission to the oral exams depends on success in these tests. The oral phase lasts as long as necessary to assess the merits of the candidate, up to a maximum of three hours. The examination commission awards a certificate to the successful candidates at the end of the exams.

II. Further training of judges and public prosecutors

The bodies responsible for the training of judges and public prosecutors in Slovenia are the Justice Ministry and the Judicial Service Commission, which is only responsible for the training of judges. Every year, they draw up a training programme for judges, public prosecutors and the other legal professions; this programme includes the topics to be treated during the year.

The most common training activities are annual seminars relating to various branches of law and to changes in the existing law. Small workshops are also organised enabling an exchange of knowledge or experience between judges or public prosecutors. Finally, courses in rhetoric and foreign languages are also offered. Attendance at these events is voluntary for judges and public prosecutors.

Moreover, the Association of law firms of the Republic of Slovenia and the Association of business lawyers of the Republic of Slovenia annually organise law days in the city of Portoroz. These days, which are open to all legal professionals, constitute the most extensive further training activity currently existing in Slovenia.

III. Reforms likely to be introduced in the near future

A reform has been recently proposed relating to admission to the office of public prosecutor: it consisted of having public prosecutors no longer appointed by the government, but, like judges, by the National Assembly. However, in the course of the debate on the question in Parliament, the Parliamentary Committee on Justice took a position against the reform, bringing an end to this attempt.

SPAIN

I. Requirements for admission to the professions of judge and public prosecutor and initial training

Two separate bodies are responsible for the recruitment of judges and public prosecutors in Spain: since the reform introduced by the Institutional Act of 8 November 1994, it is the General Council of the Judiciary which selects judges while the Justice Ministry remains in charge of the selection of public prosecutors.

Admission to both professions is based on two separate competitive entrance exams open to persons with degrees in law. However, one-quarter of the posts of judge are filled through another system; namely, a test and an interview enabling the General Council of the Judiciary to assess the merits of the candidates. This means of access to the profession of judge is open to lawyers having at least six years of professional experience.

The candidates for these two professions must have Spanish nationality, have reached the age of majority, have a diploma showing the completion of university studies in law and enjoy their civil rights. Each competitive entrance exam is made up of three tests relating to the following subjects: theory of law, constitutional law, administrative law, civil law, labour law, commercial law, criminal law, and procedure.

The candidates who are successful in this exam must then undergo a one year period of specific training organised. For judges, this training takes place at the Judicial School. It lasts two years and is organised by the General Council of the Judiciary. The initial training of public prosecutors is organised by the Justice Ministry. It takes place in public prosecutors' offices and lasts six months. However, this period may be extended to one or one and a half years next year. The training periods are made up of theoretical and practical instruction. Judges recruited directly by the General Council of the Judiciary need not undergo any specific training.

II. Further training of judges and public prosecutors

It is possible for judges and public prosecutors wishing to do so to undergo further training. The training activities, organised for judges by the General Council of the Judiciary and for public prosecutors by the Justice Ministry, relate exclusively to the field of law. There are, however, only few of them.

III. Reforms likely to be introduced in the near future

No reforms concerning the recruitment and training of judges/public prosecutors in Spain are currently on the agenda.

SWEDEN

I. Requirements for admission to the professions of judge and public prosecutor and initial training

In Sweden, there are neither competitive entrance exams nor recruitment tests for admission to the professions of judge and public prosecutor. The procedure for the recruitment of judges is the following: after having obtained a master's degree in law, candidates must seek admission as law clerks ("*notarie*") with a first instance court. The selection is made by the National Courts Administration and is primarily based on the results obtained by applicants during their studies. The persons admitted serve as law clerks for two years.

At the end of this period, the candidates for the office of judge must apply with a Court of Appeal for probationary admission as assistants ("*fiskalaspirant*"). Candidates are selected by each Court of Appeal. The candidates accepted are then employed for nine months on a trial basis, after which they become permanent assistants ("*fiskal*"). During this period, they have the opportunity to undergo theoretical instruction extending over two or three weeks aimed at teaching them procedure and the manner of conducting hearings.

The following stage for the trainee judges is to be appointed as assistant judges to a first instance court. The training period which follows is the most important. It lasts at least one year and permits the assistant judge to fully exercise judicial functions in simple cases and under his own responsibility. The exercise of his functions by each assistant judge is subject of a written evaluation.

Finally, the last stage is the appointment of the candidate as an associate judge to a Court of Appeal in order to test his skills in an appellate court.

At the end of this training period, the new judges are appointed by the Court of Appeal as temporary associate appeal judges and may exercise their functions in different courts or in other public services. They only become permanent judges upon appointment by the government, which may take place after several years of service.

Persons wishing to enter the profession of public prosecutor must make an application to the regional public prosecutor's office for a position as trainee with a local prosecutor's office. The training period is nine months, at the end of which the trainee must present a case to a jury of senior prosecutors. If the jury finds the presentation and the work during the training period satisfactory, the Prosecutor General appoints the trainee to a post of assistant district prosecutor. After three years of service in this post, the assistant district prosecutor may apply for a post as district prosecutor.

During these three years, the assistant prosecutors are required to take two courses organised by the Office of the Prosecutor General. The first is a nine week course of basic training; and the second is a three week course consisting of conferences on more specific topics. Moreover, prosecutors specialising in the law relating to economic crimes must take a special seven week course.

II. Further training of judges and public prosecutors

In Sweden, further training of judges and public prosecutors is organised by the National Courts Administration and by the Office of the Prosecutor General. It consists of conferences relating to different aspects of the law, combined with practical exercises and case studies. Also added to this are courses in foreign languages, economics, and a special training programme for presidents of courts. Each year approximately 30 to 35 events of this type are offered. Attendance is voluntary.

III. Reforms likely to be introduced in the near future

Since approximately twenty years, the opening of the office of judge to university professors, barristers and public prosecutors has been envisaged. This idea is currently being examined by the Justice Ministry.

SWITZERLAND

Preliminary remark:

As the concept of the public prosecutor does not exist in Swiss law, this concept has been understood as including both prosecutors and investigating judges. However, the answers given being applicable all judges, the distinction made in the questionnaire has not been followed here.

*
* *

I. Requirements for admission to the profession of judge and initial training

In Switzerland, judges are not recruited on the basis of a competitive examination, but they are appointed in different ways:

- federal judges and the majority of the cantonal judges and appellate judges are appointed by the legislative power, ie by the Federal Assembly or, at the cantonal level, by the High Council;

- the judges of the cantons of Geneva, Basel-City and Tessin are elected by the people;

- the judges of first instance of the cantons of Vaud and Valais are elected by the cantonal court;

- finally, in the canton of Fribourg, the judges of first instance are elected by an electoral college composed of cantonal judges and members of the government.

To be eligible, candidates for the office of judge must have Swiss citizenship (except for the canton of Basel-City where foreign professors at the faculty of law may also be elected), be admissible to the civil service and must enjoy their civil rights. Most of the cantons have the further requirement that the candidates must have university or post-university training, but this requirement is not universal. Some cantons have a minimum or maximum age limit. Finally, the Federal Assembly, responsible for the election of the federal court judges, ensures that the three official languages of the Federation are represented among the judges.

Once elected, judges are not required to undergo any specific training but they do have access to further training.

II. Further training of judges

Judges have numerous opportunities for further training at the federal level as well as at the level of the cantons.

At the federal level, the two institutions primarily responsible for further training are the Swiss Association of Judges of the Ordinary Courts, a member of the International Union of Judges and the Foundation for further training of Swiss judges. The first of these bodies has the aim of promoting and supporting further training of judges at the federal level; it also organises internships for foreign judges and establishes contacts with the cantonal judges' associations.

The second body, and the most imporant, is the Foundation for further training of Swiss judges. It was created in 1992 and has its headquarters in Bern. The Foundation's aim is "the further training of judges, registrars, prosecutors and investigating judges practising in Switzerland full- or part-time" (Art. 3 of the Founding Instrument). To this end, it organises seminars and study trips abroad. The seminars, two per year - or more if required - generally relate to subjects directly concerning the judge in the exercise of his office, such as the researching of the decision, professional technique or the administration of justice. They take place as follows: the seminar begins with a presentation of the subject chosen, followed by a discussion in groups - the number of participants in these seminars being limited -, after which a rapporteur presents the conclusions of each group in the final discussion. Attendance in these seminars and other training activities is purely voluntary for judges.

III. Reforms likely to be introduced in the near future

No reforms on the admission to the profession of judge and their training are currently in progress or envisaged in Switzerland.

"THE FORMER YUGOSLAV REPUBLIC OF MACEDONIA"

The only way of being admitted to the professions of judge or public prosecutor is by a competitive entrance exam. Candidates are selected by Parliament.

In order to be admitted to these professions, candidates must satisfy the following requirements: be a citizen of "the Former Yugoslav Republic of Macedonia", have graduated from legal studies and have passed a professional exam.

The candidates who are selected are admitted directly and permanently to the office of judge or public prosecutor. They are not required to undergo any training period and are not restricted as to the functions they may perform at the beginning of their career.

At the moment, no further training is open to judges or public prosecutors in "the Former Yugoslav Republic of Macedonia".

Nevertheless, the lacunas in the present system may be filled by future reforms and in particular by the new Law relating to the Courts, which is on the verge of being promulgated.

UKRAINE

I. Requirements for admission to the professions of judge and public prosecutor and initial training

In Ukraine, judges and public prosecutors are not recruited in the same way; contrary to the latter, the former must, in general, pass a selection examination.

In effect, even though judges are elected to their posts, they are required to pass a professional qualification exam before they can be elected for the first time. A qualification commission decides whether or not the candidate for a post of judge is capable of exercising judicial functions, on the basis of the result obtained in the exam.

Candidates for a post of judge must meet certain requirements relating to their age - they must be at least 25 or 30 years old, depending on the post they wish to hold -, to their level of studies, and to their professional experience - two or three years depending on the posts.

Judges of the ordinary courts and the military courts are elected for a first term of five years, then for a term of ten years.

Ukrainian public prosecutors are not recruited by way of a competitive examination, but are appointed by the Prosecutor General. They must meet certain requirements concerning their age and professional experience: thus district prosecutors must be at least 25 years old and have three years of professional experience, and regional prosecutors must be at least 30 years old and have seven years of professional experience.

Lawyers wishing to enter the profession of prosecutor must first undergo a one year training period with the district prosecutor's office. At the end of this training period, they go before a reference commission which decides whether or not they are suitable for the exercise of the functions of a prosecutor. If the Commission does not find them ready to exercise these functions, it may decide to extend their training period by six months before re-examining the candidacy. Those who, even after six additional months of training, are found unsuitable for the profession of prosecutor are offered another post.

II. Further training of judges and public prosecutors

It is the Justice Ministry which is responsible for further training of Ukrainian judges but this training is currently only in the process of being introduced.

Ukrainian public prosecutors are required to take courses of further training once every five years. Approximately ten courses, each one lasting between one and one and a half months are organised each year by the Prosecutor General's Office.

III. Reforms likely to be introduced in the near future

No reforms are currently envisaged in Ukraine concerning the recruitment and training of public prosecutors.

UNITED KINGDOM

The United Kingdom is a unitary state which does however have three separate legal systems, namely those of England and Wales, Scotland and Northern Ireland. This synthesis deals with the system of England and Wales only.

In England and Wales, the systems of recruitment and training of judges and "public prosecutors" are quite different. The two systems will therefore be presented separately.

A. *The training of judges*

I. Requirements for admission to the profession of judge and initial training

The judges of England and Wales are not recruited by way of a competitive examination or a similar test but are appointed from among experienced members of the legal profession. The requirements to be met and the appointment procedures differ from post to post but the Lord Chancellor has in every case a key role to play. He recommends the appointment of High Court judges to the Queen. It is the Prime Minister who in turn advises the Queen as to the appointment of the higher judiciary but this advice will not be given without taking note of the recommendations of the Lord Chancellor. The Lord Chancellor himself makes appointments to the lesser judicial posts such as that of justice of the peace.

The central criterion for the choice of the Lord Chancellor is that he must appoint or recommend the candidate who appears to him to be the best qualified to fill the vacant post, based on the candidates' integrity, legal knowledge and personal characteristics.

Appointment to the High Court bench is by invitation and not by application. No such appointment will be made unless the individual concerned has enjoyed rights of audience in courts of the appropriate level for ten years or been a Circuit judge for two years.

In July 1993, the Lord Chancellor announced his intention to make some changes in the appointment procedures. The changes envisaged included advertising for applicants for the lowest posts in the hierarchy (lower than those of the judges of the High Court).

Judges appointed for the first time must normally attend mandatory induction courses in civil and criminal law. It is however important to note that the new judges already have considerable legal experience but are appointed at first as part-time judges before being able to exercise their functions full-time. The induction courses are practical rather than theoretical in content.

The induction courses aimed at new judges are organised by the Judicial Studies Board, which was created in 1979. The induction course in criminal law lasts three and a half days, following which the new judge spends one to two weeks with a criminal judge and visits local prisons, including a youth offenders' institution and the Probation Service. The induction course in civil law lasts five days, followed by a training period with a civil court judge and a week during which the new judge is supervised in the exercise of his functions.

II. Further training of judges

The further training of judges in England and Wales is organised by the Judicial Studies Board. In criminal law, seminars are organised approximately every five years, but the interval is gradually being reduced. These seminars are intended to update the legal knowledge of the participants and include discussions and exercises. Aside from pure law, other areas are also included in the seminars such as child psychology, forensic medicine, drug-related problems and problems of racial discrimination. Seminars are also organised in civil law approximately every four years, the aim again being to increase their frequency. These seminars include conferences and discussions. Moreover, seminars are sometimes organised on other topics such as European Community Law or judicial review, when a need is perceived.

Approximately forty seminars were scheduled for 1995. Attendance is not mandatory but judges are expected to and do attend.

III. Reforms likely to be introduced in the near future

A reform relating to the structure, resources and activities of the Judicial Studies Board is currently under study and recommendations already implemented include the appointment of joint Directors of Studies.

B. *The training of "public prosecutors"*

I. Requirements for admission to the profession of "public prosecutor" and initial training

It is important to remember that the prosecution service is a recent introduction in England and Wales: the Crown Prosecution Service was set up only in 1986. Previously, prosecutions were conducted by lawyers in private practice, and in some cases, by the police. There are other bodies which conduct prosecutions such as the Serious Fraud Office.

The lawyers of the Crown Prosecution Service (hereinafter "CPS") are recruited at two levels: persons already having the qualification of barrister or solicitor may directly join the CPS on the basis of an interview. Persons not yet having one of these qualifications are recruited as legal trainees on the basis of a test consisting of the solution of a practical case followed by an interview. There is no other means of access to the CPS.

The body responsible for the selection of the candidates is a committee of three members, two of whom are senior lawyers and the third is a civil servant. To assess the candidates, the committee looks, on the one hand, at their legal knowledge and, on the other hand, at their personal characteristics.

The candidates selected in this way gain direct admission to the CPS but only solicitors and barristers may immediately become prosecutors. Trainee barristers are offered a one year contract and trainee solicitors a two year contract. This duration corresponds to the duration of their training period which they normally must serve in order to obtain one of these qualifications: thus a trainee barrister, for example, instead of serving his mandatory training period with a barrister, may serve it with the CPS.

The new members of the CPS recruited in this way must undergo training organised by the training service of the CPS which varies according to their status: prosecutors are offered different further training courses adapted to their level during the first three years of their career. The trainees first take a general seminar of five days organised at the national level and must then take courses aimed at trainee solicitors or barristers.

It is only at the end of their training period that trainees may practise as CPS prosecutors, contrary to solicitors and barristers who have no formal limit imposed on the exercise of their functions.

II. Further training of cps prosecutors

The only kind of further training for CPS prosecutors in England and Wales are the further training courses offered to them during the first three years of their careers. When a need is perceived, specialised courses are also organised in certain areas, as, for example, juvenile delinquency.

III. Reforms likely to be introduced in the near future

If, in the future, CPS prosecutors are permitted to plead in the Crown Court - which they are presently not yet allowed to do - the training service of the CPS will set up such further training schemes as appropriate.

Tab.1 : ADMISSION TO THE PROFESSIONS OF JUDGE AND PUBLIC PROSECUTOR

Countries	Competitive entrance exam	Body responsible	Type of tests	Direct admission/training	Other ways of admission
ALBANIA	no	/	/	/	/
AUSTRIA	yes	presidents of the 3 courts of Appeal + body of judges	oral and written, psycho. test, individual hearing	training	special exam for lawyers and notaries
BELARUS	no	/	/	/	/
BELGIUM	yes	Recruitment Board of Judges	oral and written	training	professional skills exam
BULGARIA	no	/	/	/	/
CROATIA	no	/	/	/	/
CYPRUS	no	/	/	/	/
CZECH REP.	no	/	/	/	/
DENMARK	no	/	/	/	/
ESTONIA	yes	Judicial Exam Commission + State Prosecutor's Office	legal tests	training for judges ; immediate admission for prosecutors	some lawyers can be exempted from the exam
FINLAND	no	/	/	/	/

Tab.1 : ADMISSION TO THE PROFESSIONS OF JUDGE AND PUBLIC PROSECUTOR					
Countries	Competitive entrance exam	Body responsible	Type of tests	Direct admission/training	Other ways of admission
FRANCE	yes	National School for the Judiciary	oral and written tests on law and general culture	training	possible exemption from the exam or from the training
GERMANY	no	/	/	/	/
GREECE	yes	National School for the Judiciary	oral and written tests on law and general culture	training	/
HUNGARY	no	/	/	/	/
ITALY	yes	commission composed of lawyers and professors	oral and written tests on law	training	/
LATVIA	no	/	/	/	/
LITHUANIA	only for judges	2 exam commissions	not specified	direct admission	/
LUXEMBOURG	no	/	/	/	/
MOLDOVA	yes	Ministry of Justice (judges[1]) State Prosecutor's Office (p)	exam (j) interview (p)	training only for inexperienced candidates	/

Tab.1 : ADMISSION TO THE PROFESSIONS OF JUDGE AND PUBLIC PROSECUTOR

Countries	Competitive entrance exam	Body responsible	Type of tests	Direct admission/training	Other ways of admission
NETHERLANDS	only for persons under 30	committee	psycho. and intelligence tests, interview	training	only for persons above 30
NORWAY	no	/	/	/	/
POLAND	yes	Presidents of courts (j) + Heads of Prosecutors' Offices (p)	tests on law	training	some applicants may be exempted from the exam
PORTUGAL	yes	Centre for Judicial Studies	tests on law and general culture	training	/
ROMANIA	no	/	/	/	/
RUSSIAN FEDERATION (j)	yes	exam commission	not specified	direct admission	/
SLOVAKIA	interview	regional courts and Prosecutors' Offices		direct admission	/
SLOVENIA	no	/	/		/

Tab.1 : ADMISSION TO THE PROFESSIONS OF JUDGE AND PUBLIC PROSECUTOR

Countries	Competitive entrance exam	Body responsible	Type of tests	Direct admission/training	Other ways of admission
SPAIN	yes	General Council of the Judiciary (j), Min. of Justice (p)	tests on law	training	test and interview
SWEDEN	no	/	/	/	/
SWITZERLAND	no	/	/	/	/
"THE FORMER YUG.REP.OF MACEDONIA"	yes	Parliament		direct admission	/
UKRAINE	only for judges	qualification commission	not specified	direct admission	/
UNITED KINGDOM	no	/	/	/	/

Tab.2 : ADMISSION TO THE PROFESSION OF JUDGE AND PUBLIC PROSECUTOR IN THE COUNTRIES IN WHICH THERE IS NO COMPETITIVE ENTRANCE EXAM

Countries	Way of admission	Body responsible	Training
ALBANIA	appointment after a test	Judicial Service Commission	yes
BELARUS	appointment or election	President of the Republic (judges[2]), Prosecutor General (p), Parliament (elects some judges and the Prosecutor General)	yes
BULGARIA	appointment	Judicial Service Commission	yes
CROATIA	appointment	National Judicial Council	no
CYPRUS	appointment	Judicial Service Commission (j), Advisory Committee (p)	no
CZECH REPUBLIC	appointment	President of the Republic (j), Minister of Justice (p)	yes
DENMARK	appointment	The Queen on the recommendation of the Min of Justice (j) or the latter on his own (p)	yes

Tab.2 : ADMISSION TO THE PROFESSION OF JUDGE AND PUBLIC PROSECUTOR IN THE COUNTRIES IN WHICH THERE IS NO COMPETITIVE ENTRANCE EXAM

Countries	Way of admission	Body responsible	Training
FINLAND	appointment	Pres.of the Rep.(j) Min.of Justice (p)	no
GERMANY	appointment or election	various bodies	yes
HUNGARY	appointment	Pres.of the Rep.(j), Principal State Prosecutor (p)	no
LATVIA	appointment	Min.of Justice or Parliament (j), Prosecutor General (p)	no, but there is an initial in-service training period
LITHUANIA (p)	appointment	Prosecutor General	yes in theory, but it has not been established yet
LUXEMBOURG	appointment after a training period in courts and an exam	Minister of Justice	yes
NETHERLANDS (persons above 30)	admission on the basis of their applications	a specific committee and the court concerned	yes
NORWAY	appointment	government	no

Tab.2 : ADMISSION TO THE PROFESSION OF JUDGE AND PUBLIC PROSECUTOR IN THE COUNTRIES IN WHICH THERE IS NO COMPETITIVE ENTRANCE EXAM

Countries	Way of admission	Body responsible	Training
ROMANIA	appointment	President of the Rep.	voluntary
SLOVAKIA	admission for initial training on the basis of an interview, then appointment (p) or election (j)	Prosecutor general (p) Parliament (j)	yes
SLOVENIA	election (j) or appointment (p)	National Assembly (j) government (p)	yes
SWEDEN	apprenticeship in courts	National Courts Administration	yes
SWITZERLAND	election	various bodies	no
UKRAINE (p)	appointment	Prosecutor General	yes
UNITED KINGDOM	appointment	various bodies	yes

Tab.3 : INITIAL TRAINING OF JUDGES AND PUBLIC PROSECUTORS

Countries	Initial training	Body responsible	Type of training	Duration of training
ALBANIA	yes	Judicial Service Commission	not specified	not specified
AUSTRIA	yes	not specified	internship in various bodies and theoretical courses	3 years
BELARUS	yes	not specified	internships	2 years (judges[3]) 6 months (p)
BELGIUM	yes	Advisory Committee	internships and courses	3 years
BULGARIA	yes	presidents of the regional courts	internship in a regional court	1 year
CROATIA	no	/	/	/
CYPRUS	no	/	/	/
CZECH REPUBLIC	yes	Institute for Further Training of Judges, courts and ps'offices	seminars, simulations and case studies	3 years
DENMARK	yes	not specified	theoretical and practical	4 years (j) 3 years (p and cc)[4]
ESTONIA	only for judges	Ministry of Justice and National Court	courses	2 to 4 days per month

Tab.3 : INITIAL TRAINING OF JUDGES AND PUBLIC PROSECUTORS

Countries	Initial training	Body responsible	Type of training	Duration of training
FINLAND	voluntary	Courts of Appeal	internship in district courts	1 year
FRANCE	yes	National School for the Judiciary	internships and courses	31 months
GERMANY	yes	not specified	internships	2 years
GREECE	yes	National School for the Judiciary	seminars and exercises	32 to 36 months
HUNGARY	no	/	/	/
ITALY	yes	Judicial Service Commission	internships and courses	2 years
LATVIA	no	/	/	/
LITHUANIA	only for judges and voluntary for some of them	Ministry of Justice	not specified	1 month
LUXEMBOURG	yes	not specified	theoretical and practical	3 years before recruitment, 1 year after
MOLDOVA	only for inexperienced candidates	not specified	internship	1 year
NETHERLANDS	yes	SSR[5]	internships and courses	6 years

Tab.3 : INITIAL TRAINING OF JUDGES AND PUBLIC PROSECUTORS

Countries	Initial training	Body responsible	Type of training	Duration of training
NORWAY	no	/	/	/
POLAND	yes	Min.of Justice, courts and prosecutors' offices	seminars and internships	2 years
PORTUGAL	yes	Centre for Judicial Studies	courses and internships	28 ½ months
ROMANIA	voluntary	National Institute for the Training of Judges	courses and internships	9 months
RUSSIAN FEDERATION (j)	no	/	/	/
SLOVAKIA	yes	not specified	theoretical and practical	judges : 3 years prosecutors : 2 years
SLOVENIA	yes	not specified	courses and internships	2 years
SPAIN	yes	General Council of the Judiciary (j) and Ministry of Justice (p)	theoretical and practical courses	judges : 2 years prosecutors : 6 months
SWEDEN	yes	National Courts Administration	apprenticeship in various courts	p : about 4 years j : 4 years at least
SWITZERLAND	no	/	/	/

Tab.3 : INITIAL TRAINING OF JUDGES AND PUBLIC PROSECUTORS

Countries	Initial training	Body responsible	Type of training	Duration of training
"THE FORMER YUG. REP. OF MACEDONIA"	no	/	/	/
UKRAINE	only for prosecutors	district prosecutors' offices	internship	1 year
UNITED KINGDOM	yes	CPS[6] (p), Judicial Studies Board (j)	courses	variable

Tab.4 : FURTHER TRAINING OF JUDGES AND PUBLIC PROSECUTORS

Countries	Further training	Body responsible	Type of activities	Number of activities organised annually	Mandatory/ voluntary participation
ALBANIA	yes	Ministry of Justice	seminars and tests	not specified	voluntary in general
AUSTRIA	yes	Ministry of Justice (among others)	courses, meetings, conferences and seminars	± 60	voluntary
BELARUS	not specified	/	/	/	/
BELGIUM	no	/	/	/	/
BULGARIA	yes	Ministry of Justice (among others)	courses	minimal 2 sessions of courses	mandatory
CROATIA	yes, but there is no permanent structure	various associations of lawyers	seminars and conferences	variable	not specified
CYPRUS	no	/	/	/	/
CZECH REPUBLIC	yes	Ministry of Justice	explanations about the implementation of new legislation	± 40	voluntary

Tab.4 : FURTHER TRAINING OF JUDGES AND PUBLIC PROSECUTORS

Countries	Further training	Body responsible	Type of activities	Number of activities organised annually	Mandatory/ voluntary participation
DENMARK	yes	Ministry of Justice	courses and seminars	1994 : 40 courses for j' variable for p	voluntary
ESTONIA	yes	various bodies	seminars, courses and workshops	j : not specified p : 4 at least	j : voluntary p : mandatory
FINLAND	yes	j: Ministry of Justice (MJ) p: MJ + Prosecutor's Office	courses	1994 : 359 days of training for judges and 30 for prosecutors	voluntary, but expected
FRANCE	yes	National School for the Judiciary	seminars, internships and bilateral exchanges	several hundreds	voluntary
GERMANY	yes	German Academy of Judges + Ministers of Justice of the *Länder*	courses	± one hundred are organised by the Academy	voluntary
GREECE	yes in theory	/	/	/	/
HUNGARY	yes	Ministry of Justice and Supreme Prosecutor's Office	conferences, seminars and courses	1994 : 24 for judges and 9 for prosecutors	mandatory

Tab.4 : FURTHER TRAINING OF JUDGES AND PUBLIC PROSECUTORS

Countries	Further training	Body responsible	Type of activities	Number of activities organised annually	Mandatory/ voluntary participation
ITALY	yes	Judicial Service Commission	meetings and seminars	± 10	voluntary
LATVIA	yes	various bodies	seminars and courses	not specified	not specified
LITHUANIA	no	/	/	/	/
LUXEMBOURG	no	/	/	/	/
MOLDOVA	yes	Ministry of Justice (j) and General Prosecutor's Office	courses and seminars	judges : 8 prosecutors : 12	mandatory
NETHERLANDS	yes	SSR[8]	courses	± 150	voluntary
NORWAY	no	/	/	/	/
POLAND	yes	Ministry of justice, voïevodship courts and prosecutors' offices	conferences, seminars and workshops	1994 : 12 at the national level and 83 at the regional level	voluntary

Tab.4 : FURTHER TRAINING OF JUDGES AND PUBLIC PROSECUTORS

Countries	Further training	Body responsible	Type of activities	Number of activities organised annually	Mandatory/ voluntary participation
PORTUGAL	yes	Centre for Judicial Studies	study sessions, colloquia and seminars	not specified	only the complementary training for new judges and prosecutors is mandatory
ROMANIA	yes	Ministry of Justice (j) and Prosecutor's Office	seminars, colloquia and workshops	judges : ± 15 prosecutors : ± 12	mandatory
RUSSIAN FEDERATION (j)	no	/	/	/	/
SLOVAKIA	yes	Ministry of Justice (j) and General Prosecutor's Office (p)	courses, seminars and international exchanges	not specified	not specified
SLOVENIA	yes	Ministry of Justice and Judicial Service Commission	seminars, workshops and courses	not specified	voluntary
SPAIN	yes	General Council of the Judiciary (j) and Min. of Justice (p)	not specified	few	voluntary

Tab.4 : FURTHER TRAINING OF JUDGES AND PUBLIC PROSECUTORS

Countries	Further training	Body responsible	Type of activities	Number of activities organised annually	Mandatory/ voluntary participation
SWEDEN	yes	National Courts Administration and Office of the Attorney General	conferences, courses and practical exercises	30 to 35	voluntary
SWITZERLAND	yes	various bodies	seminars and study visits	2 seminars per year	voluntary
"THE FORMER YUG. REP. OF MACEDONIA"A CEDONIA	no	/	/	/	/
UKRAINE	judges : it is being introduced prosecutors : yes	Ministry of Justice (j) and Office of the Attorney General (p)	courses (p)	± 10 (p)	mandatory (p)
UNITED KINGDOM	yes	Judicial Studies Board (j) and Crown Prosecution Service (p)	seminars (j) and further training courses (p)	about 40 are scheduled this year	voluntary, but expected

PROGRAMME

Thursday, 27 April 1995

09h 00   Arrival of participants

09h 30   Opening sitting chaired by the Portuguese Minister of Justice

Chairman of the session: Mr Jean-Pierre ROYER, Professor, Honorary Dean of the Faculty of Law, University of Lille II - Law and Health, France

10h 00   **Conditions of access to the profession of judge and public prosecutor - selection criteria and recruiting procedures. Comparison**

Rapporteurs:

Mr Johann-Friedrich STAATS, Chief of Service to the Federal Ministry of Justice, Bonn, Germany

Mme Ana PÉREZ TÓRTOLA, Member of the Consejo General del Poder Judicial, Madrid, Spain

Mr Fernando ESCRIBANO MORA, Secretary General of Justice, Madrid, Spain

Mr Daniel LUDET, Director of the Ecole Nationale de la Magistrature (ENM), Bordeaux, France

Mr Joep VERBURG, Director of the Stichting Sutdiecentrum Rechtspleging (SSR), Zutphen, the Netherlands

Mr Armando LEANDRO, Director of the Centro de Estudos Judiciários (CEJ), Lisbon, Portugal

Mr Ian CAMPBELL, Judge at the Court of Liverpool, United Kingdom

Mr Stanislaw WALTÓS, Professor of Law, Uniwersytet Jagielloński (UJ), Cracow, Poland

11h 30   Pause

11h 45   Discussion

13h 00   Buffet

Chairman of the session: Mr Daniel LUDET, Director of the Ecole Nationale de la Magistrature (ENM), Bordeaux, France

14h 30   **Basic training: content and methods, duration of the various phases**

Brief outline of the various systems in Western European countries

Rapporteurs:

Mrs Maud VIGNAU, Director of Basic Training at the Ecole Nationale de la Magistrature (ENM), Bordeaux, France

Mr Joep VERBURG, Director of the Stichting Studiecentrum Rechtspleging (SSR), Zutphen, the Netherlands

Mr José António MESQUITA, Director of Study at the Centro de Estudos Judiciários (CEJ), Lisbon, Portugal

16h 00   **In-service training: content, methods and evaluation of results**

Brief outline of the different systems in Western European countries

Rapporteurs:

Mr Helmut PALDER, Chief Adviser to the Ministry of Justice of Bavaria, Munich, Germany

Mr José de la MATA AMAYA, Director of Training, Consejo General del Poder Judicial, Madrid, Spain

Mr Daniel LECRUBIER, Deputy Director of the Ecole Nationale de la Magistrature (ENM) and Director of in-service training, Paris, France

Mr Joep VERBURG, Director of the Stichting Studiecentrum Rechtspleging (SSR), Zutphen, the Netherlands

Mr Armando LEANDRO, Director of the Centro de Estudos Judiciários (CEJ), Lisbon, Portugal

16h 45   Break

17h 00	Discussion
19h 00	Reception at the town hall

Friday, 28 April 1995

Chairman of the session: Mr Stanislaw WALTOŚ, Professor of Law, Uniwersytet Jagielloński (UJ), Cracow, Poland

09h 00 **Consideration of the setting up of training courses and structures in the countries of Central and Eastern Europe: current situation, projects, difficulties encountered**

Brief presentations by representatives of the countries of Central and Eastern Europe

10h 30 Break

10h 45 Discussion

13h 00 Buffet

Chairman of the session: Mr Armando LEANDRO, Director of the Centro de Estudos Judiciários (CEJ), Lisbon, Portugal

14h 30 **Prospects for co-operation between the various training bodies in Europe. Creation of a European network of training bodies**

Proposals - Conclusions

16h 00 **Closure**

LIST OF PARTICIPANTS / LISTE DES PARTICIPANTS

ALBANIA / ALBANIE

Mr Vladimir KRISTO, Vice-Minister of Justice

Mr Edison HEBA, Director of Legal Research and Foreign Relation Department, Prosecutor General's Office

AUSTRIA / AUTRICHE

M. Wolfgang JEDLICKA, Juge à la Wiener Neustadt et Vice-Président de l'Union des Juges Autrichiens

M. Gerhard REISSNER, Juge et Vice-Président de l'Union des Juges Autrichiens

BELARUS

Mr Valeri GODOUNOV, Dean of the Legal Faculty of the Belarusian State University

Mr Uladzimir SAKALOUSKI, Director, Law and Treaties Department, Ministry of Foreign Affairs

BULGARIA / BULGARIE

M. Evgueni STAIKOV, Président de la Cour de la Ville de Sofia

Mrs Petrana BANDOVA, Public Prosecutor at the Attorney General's Office

CROATIA / CROATIE

Mr Ivo GRBIN, Judge of the Supreme Court of the Republic of Croatia

Mr Ivan PLEVKO, Deputy District Public Prosecutor

CZECH REPUBLIC / REPUBLIQUE TCHEQUE

M. Vladimir STIBOŘÍK, Vice-Président de la Haute Cour de Prague aux Affaires Criminelles

Mr Zdenek SOVÁK, Chief Judge of the High Court of Prague

DENMARK/DANEMARK

Mr Mogens BEIER, Judge, member of Danish Committee on training of judges and deputy judges

Mr Ole K. DYBDAHL, Head of Department, Ministry of Justice

ESTONIA / ESTONIE

Mrs Anne LOIK, Head of Personnel Department, Ministry of Justice

Mr Indrek MEELAK, Prosecutor General, Ministry of Justice

GREECE/GRECE

M. Konstantinos MENOUDAKOS, Conseiller d'Etat et Directeur d'Etudes à l'Ecole Nationale de la Magistrature de Grèce

HUNGARY / HONGRIE

Mme Éva KISS, Juge à la Cour du Département Komárom-Esztergom

Mme Istvánné KÖRMENDY, Procureur au Parquet Général de la République de Hongrie

ITALY/ITALIE

M. Domenico CARCANO, Membre du Conseil Supérieur de la Magistrature

M. Giovanni FIANDACA, Professeur, Membre du Conseil Supérieur de la Magistrature

M. Vladimiro ZAGREBELSKY, Membre du Conseil Supérieur de la Magistrature

LATVIA / LETTONIE

Mr Uldis DZENITIS, Deputy Secretary of State, Ministry of Justice

Mr Gunars KUTRIS, Head Prosecutor, Methodology Unit, General Prosecutor's Office,

LITHUANIA / LITUANIE

M. Albertas MILINIS, Président du Tribunal de District de Kaunas, membre du Conseil des Juges

M. Vytautas MASIOKAS, Président du Tribunal de Kaunas, Président de l'Association des Juges

MOLDOVA

M. Aurel CHISTRUGA, Juge au tribunal d'arrondissement Riscani de la ville de Chisinau,

POLAND/POLOGNE

Mr Andrzej KUBA, Director of Personnel Department, Ministry of Justice

Mr Igor DZIALUK, Public Prosecutor, Legal Department, Ministry of Justice

ROMANIA / ROUMANIE

M. Gheorghe NICHITA, Premier-procureur, Parquet Général près de la Cour Suprême de Justice

M. Adrian TELU, Directeur de la Direction de l'organisation et des ressources humaines du Ministère de la Justice

RUSSIAN FEDERATION / FEDERATION DE RUSSIE

Mr Anatoly I. MURANOV, Vice-Minister of Justice, Head, Courts Department, Ministry of Justice

Mr Vladimir B. ZIMONENKO, Head, Public Relations Department, Ministry of Justice,

SLOVAK REPUBLIC / REPUBLIQUE SLOVAQUE

Mrs Eleonóra MIKULOVÁ, Institute of Law, Ministry of Justice

Mrs Lýdia ĎUROŠOVÁ, Public Prosecutor, Attorney General's Office

SLOVENIA / SLOVENIE

Mrs Janka ŠOLINC, Judge in the District Court Kranj

Mr Silvij ŠINKOVEC, Supreme State Prosecutor

SPAIN/ESPAGNE

M. Juan Ignacio CAMPOS CAMPOS, Magistrat du Parquet, membre du Secrétariat Technique du Bureau du Procureur Général

SWEDEN/SUEDE

Mr Bertil HÜBINETTE, Director General of Domstolsverket (Swedish National Courts Administration)

Mr Per BYLÉN, Head of Division, Swedish National Courts Administration

THE FORMER YUGOSLAV REPUBLIC OF MACEDONIA / L'EX-RÉPUBLIQUE YOUGOSLAVE DE MACÉDOINE

M. Dragan TUMANOVSKI, Sous-Secrétaire d'Etat au Ministère de la Justice

Mme Snežana MOJSOVA, Conseillère au Ministère de la Justice

UKRAINE

Mrs Suzanna PURIJ, Prosecutor from the Division of staff management, Ministry of Justice of Ukraine

Mr Bronislav STYCHINSKIJ, Deputy Minister of Justice

RAPPORTEURS

Mr Ian CAMPBELL - Juge à la Cour de Liverpool, Royaume-Uni

Mr Fernando ESCRIBANO MORA, Secrétaire Général de la Justice, Madrid, Espagne

Mr Armando LEANDRO - Directeur du Centro de Estudos Judiciários (CEJ), Lisbonne, Portugal

Mr Daniel LECRUBIER - Directeur adjoint de l'Ecole Nationale de la Magistrature (ENM) et Directeur de la Formation Continue, Paris, France

Mr Daniel LUDET, Directeur de l'Ecole Nationale de la Magistrature (ENM), Bordeaux, France

Mr José de la MATA AMAYA - Directeur de la Formation, Consejo General del Poder Judicial, Madrid, Espagne

Mr José António MESQUITA - Directeur d'Etudes au Centro de Estudos Judiciários (CEJ), Lisbonne, Portugal

Mme Ána-Maria PÉREZ TÓRTOLA, Membre du Consejo General del Poder Judicial, Madrid, Espagne

Mr Helmut PALDER, Chef conseiller au Ministère de la Justice de la Bavière, Munich, Allemagne

Mr Jean-Pierre ROYER, Professeur, Doyen Honoraire de la Faculté de Droit, Université de Lille II - Droit et Santé, France

Mr Joep VERBURG - Directeur du Stichting Studiecentrum Rechtspleging (SSR), Zutphen, Pays-Bas

Mr Johann-Friedrich STAATS, Chef de Service au Ministère Fédéral de la Justice, Bonn, Allemagne

Mme Maud VIGNAU - Directeur de la Formation Initiale de l'Ecole Nationale de la Magistrature (ENM), Bordeaux, France

Mr Stanisław WALTOŚ, Professeur de droit, Uniwersytet Jagielloński (UJ), Cracovie, Pologne

CENTRO DE ESTUDOS JUDICIÁRIOS

Mr Armando LEANDRO, Directeur

Mme Helena PARADA COELHO, Responsable des relations internationales

Mr José António MESQUITA, Directeur d'Etudes

Mr João DIAS BORGES, Directeur de Stages

Mme Eliana GERSÃO, Directrice du Bureau d'Etudes Juridiques et Sociales

Mme Isabel JORDÃO, Magistrat du Parquet et Maître de Conférences

Mr Joaquim LINO GONÇALVES, Secrétaire

Mme Anjos GASPAR, Secrétariat

Mme Henriqueta COSTA, Secrétariat

SECRETARIAT

Mme Gaby TUBACH, Chef de la Division de la Coopération Juridique avec les pays d'Europe Centrale et Orientale, Direction des Affaires Juridiques

Mme Danuta WIŚNIEWSKA-CAZALS, Conseillère de programme, Direction des Affaires Juridiques

Mme Sophie MEUDAL, Consultante, Direction des Affaires Juridiques

Mme Monique CHARRETON, Assistante Administrative, Direction des Affaires Juridiques

Sales agents for publications of the Council of Europe
Agents de vente des publications du Conseil de l'Europe

AUSTRALIA/AUSTRALIE
Hunter publications, 58A, Gipps Street
AUS-3066 COLLINGWOOD, Victoria
Fax: (61) 34 19 71 54

AUSTRIA/AUTRICHE
Gerold und Co., Graben 31
A-1011 WIEN 1
Fax: (43) 1512 47 31 29

BELGIUM/BELGIQUE
La Librairie européenne SA
50, avenue A. Jonnart
B-1200 BRUXELLES 20
Fax: (32) 27 35 08 60

Jean de Lannoy
202, avenue du Roi
B-1060 BRUXELLES
Fax: (32) 25 38 08 41

CANADA
Renouf Publishing Company Limited
1294 Algoma Road
CDN-OTTAWA ONT K1B 3W8
Fax: (1) 613 741 54 39

DENMARK/DANEMARK
Munksgaard
PO Box 2148
DK-1016 KØBENHAVN K
Fax: (45) 33 12 93 87

FINLAND/FINLANDE
Akateeminen Kirjakauppa
Keskuskatu 1, PO Box 218
FIN-00381 HELSINKI
Fax: (358) 01 21 44 35

GERMANY/ALLEMAGNE
UNO Verlag
Poppelsdorfer Allee 55
D-53115 BONN
Fax: (49) 228 21 74 92

GREECE/GRÈCE
Librairie Kauffmann
Mavrokordatou 9, GR-ATHINAI 106 78
Fax: (30) 13 83 03 20

HUNGARY/HONGRIE
Euro Info Service
Magyarorszag
Margitsziget (Európa Ház),
H-1138 BUDAPEST
Fax: (36) 1 111 62 16

IRELAND/IRLANDE
Government Stationery Office
4-5 Harcourt Road, IRL-DUBLIN 2
Fax: (353) 14 75 27 60

ISRAEL/ISRAËL
ROY International
PO Box 13056
IL-61130 TEL AVIV
Fax: (972) 3 546 1442

ITALY/ITALIE
Libreria Commissionaria Sansoni
Via Duca di Calabria, 1/1
Casella Postale 552, I-50125 FIRENZE
Fax: (39) 55 64 12 57

MALTA/MALTE
L. Sapienza & Sons Ltd
26 Republic Street
PO Box 36
VALLETTA CMR 01
Fax: (356) 246 182

NETHERLANDS/PAYS-BAS
InOr-publikaties, PO Box 202
NL-7480 AE HAAKSBERGEN
Fax: (31) 542 72 92 96

NORWAY/NORVÈGE
Akademika, A/S Universitetsbokhandel
PO Box 84, Blindern
N-0314 OSLO
Fax: (47) 22 85 30 53

PORTUGAL
Livraria Portugal, Rua do Carmo, 70
P-1200 LISBOA
Fax: (351) 13 47 02 64

SPAIN/ESPAGNE
Mundi-Prensa Libros SA
Castelló 37, E-28001 MADRID
Fax: (34) 15 75 39 98

Llibreria de la Generalitat
Rambla dels Estudis, 118
E-08002 BARCELONA
Fax: (34) 34 12 18 54

SWEDEN/SUÈDE
Aktiebolaget CE Fritzes
Regeringsgatan 12, Box 163 56
S-10327 STOCKHOLM
Fax: (46) 821 43 83

SWITZERLAND/SUISSE
Buchhandlung Heinimann & Co.
Kirchgasse 17, CH-8001 ZÜRICH
Fax: (41) 12 51 14 81

BERSY
Route du Manège 60, CP 4040
CH-1950 SION 4
Fax: (41) 27 31 73 32

TURKEY/TURQUIE
Yab-Yay Yayimcilik Sanayi Dagitim Tic Ltd
Barbaros Bulvari 61 Kat 3 Daire 3
Besiktas, TR-ISTANBUL

UNITED KINGDOM/ROYAUME-UNI
HMSO, Agency Section
51 Nine Elms Lane
GB-LONDON SW8 5DR
Fax: (44) 171 873 82 00

**UNITED STATES and CANADA/
ÉTATS-UNIS et CANADA**
Manhattan Publishing Company
468 Albany Post Road
PO Box 850
CROTON-ON-HUDSON, NY 10520, USA
Fax: (1) 914 271 58 56

STRASBOURG
Librairie Kléber
Palais de l'Europe
F-67075 Strasbourg Cedex
Fax: (33) 88 52 91 21

Council of Europe Publishing/Editions du Conseil de l'Europe
Council of Europe/Conseil de l'Europe
F-67075 Strasbourg Cedex
Tel. (33) 88 41 25 81 - Fax (33) 88 41 27 80